THE GREAT
BLACK MIGRATIONS

MILESTONES
IN AMERICAN HISTORY

THE ACQUISITION OF FLORIDA

THE ALAMO

ALEXANDER GRAHAM BELL
AND THE TELEPHONE

THE ATTACK ON PEARL HARBOR

THE CALIFORNIA GOLD RUSH

THE CIVIL RIGHTS ACT OF 1964

THE DONNER PARTY

THE ELECTRIC LIGHT

THE EMANCIPATION PROCLAMATION

THE ERIE CANAL

THE GREAT BLACK MIGRATIONS

THE INTERNMENT OF
JAPANESE AMERICANS
DURING WORLD WAR II

THE LOUISIANA PURCHASE

MANIFEST DESTINY

THE MONROE DOCTRINE

THE OREGON TRAIL

THE OUTBREAK OF THE CIVIL WAR

THE PONY EXPRESS

THE PROHIBITION ERA

THE RAID ON HARPERS FERRY

THE ROBBER BARONS AND
THE SHERMAN ANTITRUST ACT

THE SCOPES MONKEY TRIAL

THE SINKING OF THE USS *MAINE*

SPUTNIK/EXPLORER I

THE STOCK MARKET CRASH OF 1929

THE TRANSCONTINENTAL RAILROAD

THE TREATY OF PARIS

THE UNDERGROUND RAILROAD

THE WRIGHT BROTHERS

THE GREAT
BLACK MIGRATIONS

FROM THE RURAL SOUTH TO THE URBAN NORTH

LIZ SONNEBORN

CHELSEA HOUSE
PUBLISHERS
An imprint of Infobase Publishing

The Great Black Migrations
Copyright © 2010 by Infobase Publishing

Chelsea House
An imprint of Infobase Publishing
132 West 31st Street
New York, NY 10001

Library of Congress Cataloging-in-Publication Data

Sonneborn, Liz.
The great Black migrations : from the rural south to the urban north / Liz Sonneborn.
   p. cm. — (Milestones in American history)
Includes bibliographical references and index.
ISBN 978-1-60413-680-7 (hardcover)
1. African Americans—Migrations—History—20th century. 2. Migration, Internal—United
States—History—20th century. 3. Rural-urban migration—United States—History—20th
century—Encyclopedias. 4. Southern States—Race relations. I. Title. II. Series.

E185.6.S67 2010
973'.0496073—dc22   2009042266

Text design by Erik Lindstrom
Cover design by Alicia Post
Composition by Keith Trego
Cover printed by Yurchak Printing, Landisville, Pa.
Book printed and bound by Yurchak Printing, Landisville, Pa.
Printed in the United States of America

This book is printed on acid-free paper.

All links and Web addresses were checked and verified to be correct at the time
of publication. Because of the dynamic nature of the Web, some addresses and links
may have changed since publication and may no longer be valid.

CONTENTS

1   Seeking Refuge   1

2   In the South   10

3   Going North   23

4   Making Their Way   39

5   Building Communities   50

6   Depression and War   61

7   The Second Wave   72

8   Heading Home   86

9   The Legacy of the Great Black Migrations   97

Chronology   107

Notes   111

Bibliography   113

Further Reading   114

Index   117

Seeking Refuge

In February 1925, the *Atlantic Monthly*, then one of the leading literary magazines in the United States, published "The City of Refuge." It tells the story of King Solomon Gillis—a tall, young black man who arrives in Harlem from his native North Carolina. Gillis is a fugitive on the run. Back home, he accidentally killed a white man. In the American South of the 1920s, such a crime would likely be punished with a grisly death. Any African American who killed a white person could expect to be lynched—publicly hanged—without the benefit of a trial.

For Gillis, Harlem is a refuge from the lawless mob that wants to string him up. But it is also a refuge from an entire way of life, the only life he has ever known. In North Carolina, blacks were treated as inferiors who were expected to kowtow to their white "betters" or else suffer horrific consequences. All too often, southern African Americans also were doomed to spend their lives in brutal rural poverty, without any legal or political rights to protect them.

COMING TO HARLEM

As the story begins, Gillis, emerging from a suffocatingly over-heated subway car, gets his first look at his new home:

> Gillis set down his tan cardboard extension case and wiped his black, shining brow. Then slowly, spreadingly, he grinned at what he saw: Negroes at every turn; up and down Lenox Avenue, up and down 135th Street; big, lanky Negroes, short, squat Negroes; black ones, brown ones, yellow ones; men standing idle on the curb, women, bundle-laden, trudging reluctantly homeward, children rattle-trapping about the side-walks; here and there a white face drifting along, but Negroes predominantly, overwhelmingly everywhere. There was assur-edly no doubt of his whereabouts. This was Negro Harlem.[1]

Gillis already knows a little about Harlem, a black neigh-borhood in New York City. He has heard stories about the place from a traveling preacher and from a neighboring family, the Uggams. Their son Mouse settled there after fighting in France during World War I (1914–1918). The Uggams told Gillis that, in Harlem, African Americans lived as well as whites did in the South: "In Harlem, black was white. You had rights that could not be denied you; you had privileges, protected by law. And you had money. Everybody in Harlem had money. It was a land of plenty."[2]

Filled with excitement, Gillis stands outside on the street for a moment, trying to take in everything around him. Suddenly, he spies something he never thought he would see, something he never even knew existed: "[A] handsome brass-buttoned giant [was] directing the heaviest traffic Gillis had ever seen; halting unnumbered tons of automobiles and trucks

Harlem, a neighborhood in New York City, began as a Dutch village in 1658. A mass migration of blacks in the area began in 1904, with people settling generally around 125th Street *(pictured above)*. By 1930, a census revealed that 70 percent of central Harlem's residents were black.

and wagons and pushcarts and streetcars; holding them at bay with one hand while he swept similar tons peremptorily on with the other; ruling the wide crossing with supreme self-assurance. And he, too, was a Negro!"[3]

Coming from the South, Gillis has never seen an African American in a position of authority, much less one wearing an impressive uniform. But Gillis is even more in awe of the black policeman when he realizes that most of the vehicles around him are manned by white drivers. As the story recounts, "One of these [cars] overdrove bounds a few feet, and Gillis heard the officer's shrill whistle and gruff reproof, saw the driver's face turn red and his car draw back like a threatened pup. It was beyond belief—impossible. Black might be white, but it couldn't be that white!"[4]

HELP FROM A "FRIEND"

On the street, overwhelmed by this strange and alluring world, Gillis runs into Mouse Uggam. He promises to help Gillis with his two most pressing problems—finding a job and finding a place to live. He sets Gillis up in a "room half the size of his hencoop back home."[5] Rising up its airshaft is an overwhelming "sewer of sounds and smells" from the city outside: "cabbage and chitterlings cooking; liver and onions sizzling, sputtering; three player-pianos out-plunking each other; a man and a woman calling each other vile things; a sick, neglected baby wailing; a phonograph broadcasting blues; dishes clacking; a girl crying heartbrokenly."[6]

With Uggam's help, Gillis also finagles a job at a grocery. Soon, Uggam comes to him with a proposal. He tells Gillis he is selling "French medicine" and wants to get Gillis in on the business. Uggam will send customers holding special coupons to the grocery store, where they will exchange the coupons with Gillis for little envelopes of "medicine." For each coupon Gillis collects, Uggam promises to give Gillis a quarter. Gillis is only too happy to oblige his friend, especially when he realizes he stands to take in an extra $18 or even $20 a week.

After Gillis agrees to the deal, Uggam walks off, "[grinning] to himself as he went on his way."[7] Everything has gone according to his plan. When Uggam first saw Gillis standing on the street, thrilled by the sights of Harlem, Uggam knew he had the perfect patsy to act as a front for his drug dealing. Uggam tells his boss, a seedy nightclub owner, how "this one come up the [subway] stairs, batted his eyes once or twice, an' froze to the spot—with his mouth wide open. Sure sign he's from 'way down behind the sun and ripe f' the pluckin'."[8]

THE END OF A DREAM

One night Gillis meets Uggam at the club to exchange his coupons for quarters. Looking around the smoke-filled room, Gillis spies a young woman dancing. He recognizes her as a beautiful woman he admired on his first day in the city. Gillis confides in Uggam that there are only two things he really wants in the world—to get a woman like that and to become a policeman like the one he saw directing traffic.

In the middle of their conversation, a white man approaches Gillis and Uggam. He pulls out a policeman's badge and tells Gillis that he is under arrest for peddling drugs. When the detective asks Uggam if he knows Gillis, Uggam relies, "Nope. Never saw him before tonight."[9]

Gillis cannot believe what is happening. In a panic, his mind wildly jumps from thought to thought: "Mouse Uggam, his friend. Harlem. Land of plenty. City of refuge—city of refuge."[10] Everyone and everything that once seemed to hold such promise has betrayed him. Gillis fights his arrest until another policeman—a black policeman—arrives to subdue him. On seeing the uniformed black man, the symbol of all his hopes, Gillis ends his struggle: "Very slowly King Solomon's arms relaxed; very slowly he stood erect; and the grin that came over his features had something exultant about it."[11]

STORIES OF THE CITY

"The City of Refuge" was the first published work written by Rudolph Fisher. When it appeared, he had just completed medical school. In just a few years, he would become renowned both in the fields of medicine and literature. Fisher also would emerge as an important figure in the Harlem Renaissance—a cultural movement of African-American writers and intellectuals based in Harlem during the 1920s and early 1930s.

Fisher's stories and novels were popular with both black and white readers. Yet his interest in depicting the lives of working-class African Americans earned him criticism from W. E. B. Du Bois, who was then one of the most famous African-American scholars in the United States. Du Bois wanted Fisher to write about people more like Fisher himself—highly educated, intelligent, and successful African-American professionals. By portraying the lives of upper-class blacks, Du Bois argued, the author could inspire impoverished African Americans and educate bigoted white Americans.

As a writer, however, Fisher preferred to explore the daily dramas he saw enacted on the streets of Harlem. He liked to write about African Americans who, despite high aspirations, had to struggle just to get by. In Harlem, at the time, many of those people were like King Solomon Gillis—southerners who had only recently arrived in the North. They were part of a phenomenon known as the Great Migration. Between 1915 and 1930, about 1.25 million southern African Americans, mostly from rural areas, left their homes to move to cities in the northern United States. Their destinations included Chicago, Illinois; Detroit, Michigan; Cleveland, Ohio; and New York, New York.

ESCAPING THE SOUTH

Like Gillis, many migrants were both running from something and running to something. Although few were literal fugitives like Fisher's character, they often were eager to escape the legal system in the South and the miseries it inflicted on black citizens. By law, African Americans were denied access to institutions, such as hospitals and schools, that were used by whites. African Americans also had few legal rights. Whites could assault and even kill blacks with little fear of being tried or imprisoned.

Following the end of the Civil War and the emancipation of the slaves, there were still an estimated 90 percent of African Americans living in former slave states. Conditions were dismal, with families living in their run-down former slave homes, and they had little opportunity to raise themselves out of poverty.

Discriminatory laws helped perpetrate a social and economic system that kept southern blacks down. Most African Americans in the South lived in poverty without any hope of bettering their lot. The few who managed to obtain an education or excel in a profession risked becoming victims of violence by white neighbors who did not want to see African Americans rise above their lowly station.

Black southerners not only wanted to escape the South. They also wanted to experience the freedom and opportunities of the North. During World War I, European migration to the United States slowed dramatically. As a result, industries in the North suffered a labor shortage and began to welcome workers from the South. News about the new opportunities for blacks in the North trickled into the southern United States. As with Gillis, a story told by a friend or even by a passing stranger often was enough to persuade black southerners to leave their homeland for a brand-new life in the North.

A LAND OF PLENTY

Gillis's vision of the northern city as a fabulous "land of plenty" was common among migrants, especially in the early years of the Great Migration. But by 1925, when Fisher's story was published, this dream of an idyllic North already had begun to fade. Like Gillis, many migrants quickly learned through bitter experience that northern cities were not the promised land they longed for. They realized they had escaped the horrors of the segregated South only to find themselves adrift and vulnerable in their new home. Far away from the support of friends and kin, migrants sometimes struggled just to survive the harsh and often brutal realities of city life.

The Great Migration came to an end with the Great Depression. This severe economic downturn in the 1930s dried up virtually all employment opportunities in the North. By about 1940, however, improving economic conditions initiated a second wave of migration—one that would last twice as long as the first and would involve more than three times the number of migrants. By the end of the Second Great Migration in about 1970, this wave had brought some 4.5 million African-American southerners north.

Together, the Great Migration and the Second Great Migration comprise one of the pivotal events in the history of twentieth-century America. The migrations transformed the demographic makeup of the United States; altered the character of American city life; and profoundly influenced American art, music, and popular culture. But they had their greatest effect on the millions of migrants and their descendants. As a result of the migrations of the twentieth century, the lives of African Americans in both the North and the South were changed forever.

In the South

Long before the twentieth century, African Americans viewed the North as a haven, far from the harsh realities of their lives in the South. Certainly, before the Civil War (1861–1865), many enslaved blacks dreamed of escaping to freedom in northern states where slavery was illegal. Only a small percentage, however, succeeded in reaching the North.

The Emancipation Proclamation granted all slaves their freedom in 1863. After the war, southern African Americans suddenly had the ability to move freely throughout the United States. In the decades that followed, some decided to migrate north. Major cities such as New York, New York; Chicago, Illinois; and Philadelphia, Pennsylvania, were popular destinations.

The vast majority, however, remained in the South. Many simply had no choice. Traveling north was an expensive proposition that most newly emancipated African Americans could scarcely afford. But they also stayed because the South was their home. Despite the bitter memories of slavery, they wanted to build their new lives as free people in the towns and farmlands they knew best and among the family and friends they loved.

THE RECONSTRUCTION ERA

With the abolition of slavery, blacks also had reason to believe that the South would undergo a radical change and become far more welcoming to its African-American population. The U.S. government enacted a set of policies, known as Reconstruction, that were intended to help rebuild the Union. One of the priorities of Reconstruction was to aid ex-slaves in the South.

Toward this end, in 1865, Congress established the Bureau of Refugees, Freedmen, and Abandoned Lands, which became known as the Freedmen's Bureau. This federal agency provided food, clothing, and medical care to impoverished black southerners. It also created schools for former slaves and provided them protection from violence perpetrated by whites. In 1875, Congress passed another important act that dealt with the rights of African Americans. The Civil Rights Act prohibited hotels, theaters, railroads, and other public facilities from discriminating against anyone on the basis of race.

During the Reconstruction era, the federal government also amended the U.S. Constitution to redefine the status of African Americans. The Thirteenth Amendment (passed in 1865) abolished slavery throughout the United States. The Fourteenth Amendment (1868) extended citizenship to ex-slaves. And the Fifteenth Amendment (1870) affirmed the right of male citizens to vote regardless of their "race, color, or previous condition of servitude." As a result, 16 black men from the South were elected to Congress during Reconstruction.

THE RISE OF JIM CROW

Despite these new constitutional protections, southern whites resisted Reconstruction policies. Already demoralized by their

Jim Crow, the legal and customary system that enforced racial segregation, mandated that public facilities and spaces would be "separate but equal." In reality, "colored only" services and accommodations were inferior to those provided to whites. Jim Crow also encompassed discrimination in employment and housing and disenfranchisement through poll taxes and literacy tests. Signs such as the one pictured were daily reminders to blacks of their unequal status.

defeat in the Civil War, they were determined to maintain their legal and social superiority over their former slaves. Southern states began instituting laws that eroded the status of their African-American residents. The system of institutionalized discrimination that emerged in the late nineteenth century was popularly called Jim Crow. The name came from a character played by white entertainer Thomas "Daddy" Rice. During the 1830s, he rose to fame in minstrel shows—entertainments in which actors, who were usually white, performed songs, dances, and skits featuring grotesque stereotypes of African Americans.

Many Jim Crow laws were designed to keep blacks and whites separate in nearly every sphere. They called for the two races to have different schools, hospitals, theaters, train cars, water fountains, bathrooms, and other public facilities. This type of racial segregation was validated by the U.S. Supreme Court in its ruling in *Plessy v. Ferguson* (1896). The case was brought by Homer A. Plessy, an African American who was arrested after sitting in a whites-only railroad car. Plessy held that the Jim Crow law that led to his arrest violated the Fourteenth Amendment. The Court disagreed. It found that African Americans' rights were not infringed upon by segregated facilities as long as the facilities for blacks were equal to those for whites.

The Court's ruling allowed racial segregation to flourish in the South well into the twentieth century. During this period, however, the accommodations for blacks and whites were rarely equal in quality. Blacks had to deal with hospitals that lacked necessary equipment and train cars that were filthy and crowded. Perhaps worst of all were the conditions in black-only schools. Southern states slashed funds for schools for African-American children, ensuring that generations of southern blacks would receive a far inferior education than that available to whites.

SUNSET TOWNS

In the South, whites also dictated where blacks could live. Many towns and cities passed ordinances prohibiting blacks from dwelling within their borders. Blacks were permitted to enter these areas, usually to work menial jobs, only during the day. Signs were posted that warned blacks not to let the sun go down on them while they were within the city limits. As a result, these all-white areas were called sunset towns.

In order to pass discriminatory laws, southern whites had to make sure that blacks were excluded from state and local politics. They did this by limiting African Americans' ability to vote. Local governments interfered with black voting rights by instituting property requirements that land-poor African Americans could not meet, by administering literacy tests that uneducated blacks could not pass, and by levying poll taxes that impoverished African Americans could not pay.

While these measures clearly were unconstitutional, white politicians in the North were content to look the other way. Since the late 1870s, most northerners had lost interest in the reforms that characterized the Reconstruction era. Many northerners, even those who had opposed slavery, considered African Americans to be inferior to whites. With such prejudices so firmly entrenched, there was little sustained desire to push for even basic civil rights for African Americans in either the North or the South.

RACIAL VIOLENCE

Southern African Americans not only were oppressed by racist laws, but they also were victims of violence organized by whites. Blacks who tried to vote, who succeeded in a profession, or who merely did not show enough deference to whites often were attacked and even killed.

This white-on-black violence was common in the late nineteenth century, but it grew even more prevalent in the first decades of the twentieth century. This era saw the rise of the Ku Klux Klan (KKK), a secretive terrorist organization founded during Reconstruction. Members of the KKK were white supremacists who used violence to cow blacks into complete submission. Wearing white masks to conceal their identity, Klansmen often burned crosses near the houses of blacks they wanted to intimidate. They sometimes kidnapped, beat, and mutilated African Americans they deemed too "uppity" in their dealings with whites.

Blacks also were terrorized by lynchings. These were public executions, usually hangings. Lynching victims often were accused of committing a crime against a white person, though often the accusation was completely false. An angry mob would

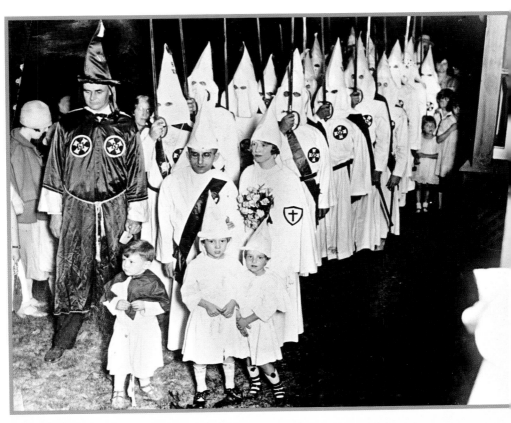

Many blacks were motivated to leave the South due to the threats and violence they faced daily. In 1865, the Ku Klux Klan (also known as the KKK, or the Klan) was founded by a group of former soldiers of the Confederate army who wanted to restore white supremacy after their defeat in the Civil War. This hate organization is on record as using terrorism, lynchings, and intimidation to oppress non-whites, Jews, Roman Catholics, and labor unions.

overpower the accused and then string him or her up as a crowd gathered to watch. Lynchings were almost social events. Women and children often were among their audiences. Onlookers frequently took photographs to commemorate the event. Postcards featuring photos of lynchings were popular souvenirs throughout the South.

THE LIFE OF SHARECROPPERS

Even for African Americans lucky enough to evade murderous mobs and the KKK, daily existence in the South often

THE BURNING OF JIM MCILHERRON

Founded in 1909, the National Association for the Advancement of Colored People (NAACP) launched a campaign to expose the horrors of lynching in the South. In the May 1918 issue of *The Crisis*, a magazine published by the NAACP, Walter F. White wrote this chilling account of the torture and murder of Jim McIlherron, an African American who had shot three white men during an argument. McIlherron was burned at the stake at the hands of an angry white mob in Estill Springs, Tennessee.

On reaching the spot chosen for the burning, McIlherron was chained to a hickory tree. The wood and other inflammable material already collected was saturated with coal oil and piled around his feet. The fire was not lighted at once, as the crowd was determined "to have some fun with the damned n—" before he died. A fire was built a few feet away and then the fiendish torture began. Bars of iron, about the size of an ordinary poker, were placed in the fire and heated to a red-hot pitch. A member of the mob took one of these and made as if to burn the Negro in the side. McIlherron seized the bar and as it was jerked from his grasp all of the inside of his hand came with it, some of the skin roasting on the hot iron. The awful stench of burning flesh rose into the air, mingled with the lustful cries of the mob and the curses of the suffering Negro. . . . Another rod was heated and, as McIlherron squirmed in agony, thrust through the flesh of his thigh, and a few minutes later another through the calf of his leg. Meanwhile, a larger bar had been heating, and while those of the

was crushing. During Reconstruction, the federal government promised to provide ex-slaves with land to start their own farms. But when it did not make good on this promise,

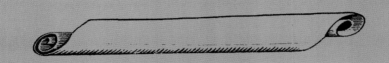

mob close enough to see shouted in fiendish glee, this was taken and McIlherron was unsexed.

The unspeakable torture had now been going on for about twenty minutes and the Negro was mercifully getting weaker and weaker. The mob seemed to be getting worked up to a higher and higher state of excitement. The leaders racked their brains for newer and more devilish ways of inflicting torture on the helpless victim.

The newspapers stated that McIlherron lost his nerve and cringed before the torture, but the testimony of persons who saw the burning is to the effect that this is untrue. . . . The only signs of the awful agony that he must have suffered were the involuntary groans that escaped his lips, in spite of his efforts to check them, and the wild look in his eyes as the torture became more and more severe. At one time, he begged his torturers to shoot him, but this request was received with a cry of derision at his vain hope to be put out of his misery. His plea was answered with the remark, "We ain't half through with you yet, n—."

By this time, however, some of the members of the mob had, apparently, become sickened at the sight and urged that the job be finished. . . . Finally, one man poured coal oil on the Negro's trousers and shoes and lighted the fire around McIlherron's feet. The flames rose rapidly, soon enveloping him, and in a few minutes McIlherron was dead.*

---

*Walter F. White, "The Burning of Jim McIlherron: An N.A.A.C.P. Investigation," *The Crisis*, May 1918, pp. 19–20, Available online at http://www.inmotionaame.org/texts/viewer.cfm?id=8_006BT&page=16.

the dream of being an independent farmer was replaced with the nightmare of being a sharecropper. By the sharecropping system, white landowners offered small tracts to landless black farmers. In exchange, the farmers gave the landowners half (and sometimes more) of the crops they produced. The farmers were left with so little for their labor that their families could barely survive. Often, they had to borrow to buy the supplies needed to keep their farms going, pulling them into a demoralizing spiral of debt and dependence. In his book *12 Million Black Voices*, Richard Wright described the sharecropper's plight:

> [W]e present ourselves to the Lord of the Land and ask to make a crop. We sign a contract—usually our contracts are oral—which allows us to keep one-half of the harvest after all debts are paid. . . . The Lords of the Land assign us ten or fifteen acres of soil already bled of its fertility through generations of abuse. . . . If we have been lucky the year before, maybe we have saved a few dollars to tide us through the fall months, but spring finds us begging an "advance"—credit— from the Lords of the Land.[1]

Nature also dealt a cruel blow to black farmers in the early years of the twentieth century. A tiny insect known as the boll weevil moved from Mexico into Texas and then into cotton-growing country throughout the South. The little boll weevil destroyed countless acres of cropland in its path. In 1915 and 1916, widespread floods spoiled any crops the boll weevil had not. Vulnerable in the best of times, sharecroppers found themselves even further impoverished in the wake of these natural disasters.

THE EXODUSTERS

As their social, economic, and legal situation in the South deteriorated, some African Americans came to feel they had no future in the region. One was Benjamin "Pap" Singleton.

B. Singleton & S. A. McClure

After the end of Reconstruction, Benjamin "Pap" Singleton, an abolitionist and former slave, organized the movement of thousands of black colonists, known as Exodusters, out of the South. They founded settlements in Kansas, a state reputed to be more progressive and tolerant than most. This photograph depicts a steamboat full of Exodusters, with Singleton and S.A. McClure, one of his associates, superimposed in the foreground.

Singleton had been a slave who, after several attempts, escaped to Canada. After the Civil War, he returned to his native Tennessee, where he worked as a carpenter. Determined to improve not only his own life but also those of other struggling former slaves, in 1874 he began circulating a poster with the title "The Advantage of Living in a Free State." Singleton's poster encouraged southern blacks to move to Kansas and establish their own farms there. Symbolically, Kansas had great meaning to

African Americans. In the years preceding the Civil War, the state had been a hotbed of antislavery activism. Its reputation made it easy for blacks to see Kansas as a land of freedom.

With a partner, Singleton formed a company that brought hundreds of African Americans from Tennessee to Kansas. But the migration he advocated grew far larger. By 1879, about 50,000 blacks had left the South and had relocated to Kansas, Missouri, Indiana, and Illinois. The migrants became known as Exodusters. The nickname referred to the biblical book of Exodus, which tells the story of Moses leading the Hebrews out of Egypt and into the Promised Land where they could be free.

In the 1890s, Oklahoma Territory also became a destination for southern blacks looking for a better life. The area had been the western portion of Indian Territory, but under pressure from Americans wanting access to farmland, the United States opened it up for non-Native settlement in 1889. Blacks as well as whites participated in the famous Oklahoma land rush and were able to claim ownership to plots there. By 1900, African-American farmers owned about 1.5 million acres (607,000 hectares) of land in Oklahoma Territory.

Developers also created dozens of towns for African-American migrants in what is now Oklahoma. The most famous was Boley, which was founded in 1904. It eventually had a population of about 1,000, with another 2,000 people living close by. In 1905, Booker T. Washington, a famous educator who was a leading national spokesman for African Americans, praised Boley as a "rude, bustling, Western town . . . which shall demonstrate the right of the negro . . . to have a worthy and permanent place in the civilization that the American people are creating."[2]

Boley did not remain bustling for long. When Oklahoma became a state in 1907, it adopted a constitution similar to those in southern states. Blacks lost any hope for political power in Oklahoma and soon found themselves living in the kind of segregated society they had taken pains to flee. Migrants to Kansas and nearby northwestern states also grew disillusioned. In addition to dealing with poor-quality land and crop-destroying blizzards, they were forced by white neighbors into sunset towns like those in the South.

LOOKING TO LIBERIA

The dream of the Exodusters faded, but the idea of migration still intrigued many southern African Americans. Convinced that they would always face discrimination in the United States, some began to imagine a new life outside its borders. A few moved to Canada and Mexico, but the most popular foreign destination was the African country of Liberia. Liberia was founded in the early 1800s by the American Colonization Society. This group, which included both slave owners and antislavery reformers, wanted to send free blacks to live in Africa. The society was largely motivated by the racist assumption that whites and blacks could never coexist in peace.

In the late nineteenth century, however, some prominent African Americans began promoting migration to Liberia as a means of escaping the Jim Crow South. The most notable was Henry McNeal Turner, a bishop in the African Methodist Episcopal Church who served in the legislature of Georgia in the 1860s. Embittered by the failure of Reconstruction, Turner formed the International Migration Society to encourage what became known as "emigrationism." The society sent several hundred migrants to Liberia in the 1890s, but the experiment proved disappointing. Several migrants returned to the United States disillusioned with Liberia because of its struggling economy and unhealthy living conditions. Their reports discouraged any widespread interest in Turner's emigrationist theories.

In the early years of the twentieth century, southern African Americans found themselves in a nearly impossible position. If they stayed in the South, they were doomed to suffer the everyday indignities of segregation with little hope of ever attaining the economic and political power to change their lives or the lives of their children. If they had the will and the means to leave the South, however, there was nowhere to go that would guarantee them a better future. Unlike Moses and his followers, for southern blacks of this period, there seemed to exist no Promised Land.

Going North

In the spring of 1916, thousands of African-American laborers from the South headed north to work for the Pennsylvania Railroad Company. The company was desperate for workers to help construct rail lines. Recruiters from the Pennsylvania Railroad actively sought out southern blacks as employees. They wanted to take advantage of the fact that, with the South's farming industry in crisis, many blacks were unemployed. The recruiters knew that these desperate African-American workers would be happy to accept wages lower than what the railroad paid white laborers.

This stream of African Americans moving north might have gone largely unnoticed if it had stopped there. Instead, it was the beginning of a much larger phenomenon. Although they had no idea of it at the time, these railroad workers were a new type of American pioneer. Their journey would inspire other southern blacks to make the trip north. Hundreds of migrants turned into thousands, and then millions, as more and more blacks decided to follow their lead. For these people, migration to the North not only promised a better income than they could find in the South. It also held the possibility of a freer and more exciting life.

WORLD WAR I AND NORTHERN INDUSTRY

Southern blacks had long had job opportunities in the North. The work available to them, however, was not very appealing. They were hired only for low-paying service jobs. Leaving one's home and family to head north to work as a maid, waiter, laundress, or elevator operator was not an attractive option for most southern blacks. Also, their chances of landing a more lucrative job in manufacturing were slim. African Americans often were blocked from this type of work by unions, worker organizations that wanted to preserve higher-paying jobs for white union members.

This situation began to change after 1914. That year saw the outbreak of World War I in Europe. Although at first the United States was not directly involved in the war, it had an immediate impact on American industry. The United States's European allies suddenly had an enormous need for weapons and other war supplies. As a result, American factories had more orders than they could fill.

At the time, only about 15 percent of factories were located in the South. The majority of American manufacturing took place in a handful of states in the North. In the Northeast, New York, Pennsylvania, New Jersey, and Massachusetts were industrial powerhouses. In the Midwest, Illinois, Michigan, Ohio, Indiana, and Wisconsin were the most important manufacturing centers.

As American industry expanded because of World War I, factories became desperate for workers. In the past, they could count on the steady stream of new immigrants from Europe to meet their employment needs. But with the outbreak of the war,

"Oakite"
Oakley Chemical Co.
New York.
43

Copyright 1917
OAKLEY CHEMICAL CO
New York

The labor shortage in the United States during World War I led to the recruitment of black workers in large numbers. By this time, some advances had been made by black males in the automobile and steel production industries. Above, men make munitions for the war on the factory floor of the Oakley Chemical Company in New York in 1917.

European immigration dropped dramatically. For instance, in 1900 about one million Europeans came to live in the United States. In 1915, the number dropped to just 350,000.

RECRUITING BLACK WORKERS

To keep up with their escalating work orders, American factories had to look elsewhere for new laborers. Racial prejudice previously had kept factories from hiring blacks, but now the potential to make big profits overrode any other concern. For the first time, factories were willing to hire blacks in great numbers. Not only were African Americans a large untapped labor source, but they also were willing to work for less money than white Americans available for factory jobs.

At the beginning of World War I, about 90 percent of African Americans still lived in the South. If northern industries were going to add blacks to their workforce, they had to find a way to encourage southern African Americans to move. Northern companies turned to labor agents, who traveled to the South to recruit black workers.

Labor agents had to be careful not to anger southern whites. Even though they generally looked down on blacks, many whites did not want to see them head north. Blacks provided southern farmers and business owners with a large pool of very inexpensive workers. Southerners knew their economy would suffer if there were fewer African-American laborers to exploit. As a result, whites did their best to thwart the agents' recruitment efforts. They tried to drive the labor agents from their communities. Sometimes, white crowds even pulled recruited workers off trains to prevent them from leaving.

To avoid the wrath of whites, agents usually worked in secret. They headed to cities, where it was easier to blend into the crowd. There, they often wandered down busy streets, whispering to African-American passersby, "Anybody who wants to go north, see me."

Labor agents were paid a fee for each recruit, so they tried to sign up anyone they could. But they were especially on the lookout for young, healthy men. They promised these prized workers high wages if they agreed to sign a work contract. Agents also often provided the most attractive recruits with a one-way railroad ticket north.

NEWS FROM THE NORTH

News quickly spread throughout the South that there were good jobs to be had in the North. Newspapers run by whites tried to counteract the rumors. Articles said that the reports about the North were exaggerated. Hoping to comfort southern whites worried about an African-American labor shortage, the papers claimed that all blacks who left would soon return, disappointed by a lack of employment options and dispirited by the cold northern winters.

Black-run newspapers in the South were almost as pessimistic about life in the North. Most of these papers were small, unprofitable, and timid about upsetting white powerbrokers. They encouraged their readership to ignore the agents and dismiss the idea of migrating. Instead, they told their readers to stay in the South and devote their energy to improving conditions for African Americans there.

For instance, the *Atlanta Independent* published an article on May 26, 1917, titled "Don't Leave—Let's Stay Home." It encouraged blacks to remain in the South while also imploring whites to give African Americans a reason to stay:

> This is our home and we do not want to leave—and we are not going to leave, unless we are driven by want and a lack of freedom from our native haunts, and we appeal to the white man who rules the country, who owns a greater part of its wealth, material and immaterial—not to drive us away but to open the doors of the shops, of the industries and the fields to our genius and push.[1]

THE *CHICAGO DEFENDER*

This message was very different from the one southern African-American readers were getting from another important news source—the *Chicago Defender*. Founded in 1905 by Robert S. Abbott, the *Defender* aimed to serve not only the African-American population of the city of Chicago, but that of the entire United States. There were other black-owned newspapers with a national audience, including the *Amsterdam News* based in New York, New York, and the *Pittsburgh Courier* based in Pittsburgh, Pennsylvania. But no newspaper

(continues on page 30)

"BOUND FOR THE PROMISED LAND"

The *Chicago Defender*, the largest black-owned newspaper in the United States, helped spur on the Great Migration by touting the advantages of living in the North to its southern black readers. Characteristic of the paper's pro-migration stance is this poem, "Bound for the Promised Land," which was published in the *Defender* on January 13, 1917. The poem's narrator celebrates his decision to leave Florida and head north. He is just as excited to escape Jim Crow laws and "Crackers" (a derogatory term for southern whites) as he is to experience the promised freedom of "Yankee Land." In keeping with the *Defender*'s editorial position, he also commands the reader to "hold up your head with courage brave" and join him on the great journey north.

From Florida's stormy banks I go;
I've bid the South "Good by";
No longer shall they treat me so,
And knock me in the eye.
The northern states is where I'm bound.
My cross is more than double—
If the chief executive can be found.
I'll tell him all my trouble.

Thousands have gone on there before,
And enjoyed their northern lives;
Nothing there they can deplore,
So they wrote back for their wives.
Thousands more now wait to go
To join the glorious sop.
The recruiters failed to take one more
Because the "Crackers" made 'em stop.

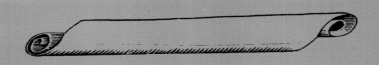

Arise! ye Darkies now a-slave
Your chance at last has come;
Hold up your head with courage brave,
'Cause times are changing some,
God is punctual to his word,
Faithful to his dating;
Humble prayers is what he heard,
After years of faithful waiting.

All before this change was made
They took me for a tool.
No respect to me was paid—
They classed me for a fool.
For centuries past I was knocked and cuffed,
And imposed upon by southern "whites";
For fifty years they had me bluffed
And robbed me of my "rights." . . .

Hasten on, my dark brother,
Duck the "Jim Crow" laws.
No "Crackers" north to slap your mother
Or knock you in the jaw.
No "Crackers" there to seduce your sister,
Nor hang you to a limb,
And you're not obliged to call them mister,
Nor show your teeth at them.

Now, why should I remain longer south,
To be kicked and dogged around?

(continues)

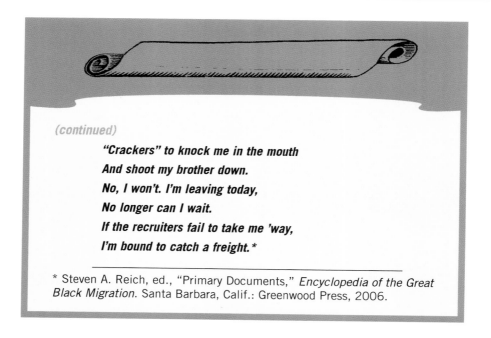

(continued)

> *"Crackers" to knock me in the mouth*
> *And shoot my brother down.*
> *No, I won't. I'm leaving today,*
> *No longer can I wait.*
> *If the recruiters fail to take me 'way,*
> *I'm bound to catch a freight.**

---

* Steven A. Reich, ed., "Primary Documents," *Encyclopedia of the Great Black Migration*. Santa Barbara, Calif.: Greenwood Press, 2006.

(continued from page 27)
would have a greater influence over the Great Migration than the *Defender*.

Like other successful papers of the era, the *Defender* favored a dramatic writing style, sensational headlines, and sordid stories about sex scandals and brutal crimes. But Abbott also used the paper to draw attention to African-American issues other publications preferred to ignore, such as lynchings and other atrocities and indignities suffered by blacks in the South. After 1916, the publisher became especially focused on another crusade—encouraging southern African Americans to seek a better life in the North.

The *Chicago Defender* gained the trust of many southern blacks by publishing article after article detailing the difficulties they faced every day in a racist society. These African Americans were not in a position to complain publicly, for fear of retaliation by whites. Reading the *Defender's* accurate and sympathetic portrayal of their struggles, therefore, encouraged southern readers to believe the paper's accounts of what awaited them up north.

THE EXCITING NORTH

The *Defender* not only described the northern labor market in rosy terms, it also talked glowingly about the quality of life in black communities in the North. There, southern blacks would be free from Jim Crow laws and no longer have to worry about lynchings. But the fact that they could benefit from institutions and commercial enterprises established by northern blacks was even more intriguing. There were black-owned stores, churches, and employment offices already in place to help southerners adjust to their new surroundings.

Just as enticing were the *Defender*'s descriptions of entertainments northern cities offered. Would-be migrants were excited by accounts of theaters with musicals and films featuring black performers, baseball games played by all-black teams, and wild nightclubs presided over by the best African-American musicians.

But the *Defender* went beyond depicting the North as a place where African Americans could make money and find exciting ways to spend it. The newspaper appealed to readers' desire to be a part of something big and important. It called the migration the "Great Northern Drive" and the "Second Emancipation."[2] These names were designed to make people think that, if they joined the migration, they were not just trying to better their lives but also were participating in an important historical event.

Southern whites were just as disturbed by the *Defender*'s campaign as they were by the work of labor agents. They tried to keep the paper from reaching southern black readers. In Alabama, two people were killed for just attempting to distribute the paper.

The *Defender* developed clever strategies for sneaking the paper into the South. Its vendors smuggled copies wrapped

By the beginning of World War I, the *Chicago Defender* was the most influential newspaper of black America. The newspaper used its influence to sway opinions and to fight injustice. It also used editorials, job postings, and articles to encourage southern blacks to migrate to the North in record numbers. In this picture, a newsboy sells copies of the *Defender* on a corner in Chicago.

in packaging that hid its contents. The paper also enlisted the help of black train porters (baggage carriers) to carry bales of the newspaper on their routes between Chicago and southern cities. With the porters' help, the *Defender* achieved a nationwide circulation. According to Abbott, by 1918, he sold 125,000 copies a week, with the majority purchased outside of the Chicago area. The number of people who read the paper was undoubtedly far higher. Friends and family passed around each copy, and the paper often was read out loud in churches and other gathering places.

ASKING FOR HELP

As more southern blacks became interested in migrating, northern employers hired fewer labor agents and rarely offered the incentive of a free railroad ticket. Increasingly, they instead placed advertisements in black newspapers, especially the *Defender*. In response to these advertisements and the *Defender*'s welcoming articles, many would-be migrants wrote to the paper asking for help.

In a letter dated April 27, 1917, a woman in Alabama politely touted her work experience cleaning laundry:

Sir: Your advertisement appearing in the *Chicago Defender* have influenced me to write to you with no delay. For seven previous years I bore the reputation of a first class laundress in Selma. . . . I have an eager desire of a clear information how to get a good position. . . . You will do me a noble favor with an answer in the earliest possible moment with a description all about the work.[3]

The next month, a man from Miami, Florida, wrote the *Defender* about the rumors he had heard of jobs in the North: "[P]eople [are] saying that all we have been hearing was false until I caught hold of the *Chicago Defender* I see where its more positions are still open. Now I am very anxious to get up there." He added that he had been a dockworker with "150 to 200 men under my charge," but said he was "willing to do anything."[4]

For one ambitious 15-year-old from Palestine, Texas, contacting the *Defender* was his first step in trying to start a new career in the North:

> I am a colored Boy aged 15 years old and I am talented for an artist . . . I have studied Cartooning . . . and I intend to visit Chicago this summer and I want . . . from you knowledge can a Colored boy be an artist and make a white man's salary up there.[5]

WRITING HOME

Both labor agents and the black press played significant roles in promoting the Great Migration. But even more important were the letters sent back to the South by the first migrants to travel north. For many people, fantastic claims from white agents and exciting promises from black reporters were easy to dismiss as exaggerations or even lies. But letters from friends and loved ones singing the praises of the North had to be taken far more seriously. They told intriguing stories about life in cities in the North. Some concentrated on the high wages migrants could expect. Others focused on the freedoms they enjoyed in the North and the relatively decent treatment blacks could expect from whites there. Perhaps the most impressive letters were ones that included gifts of money. Those letters proved that a prosperous future could indeed be had in the North.

Letters from migrants were passed from friend to friend, increasing their impact. The letters of one woman originally from Hattiesburg, Mississippi, depicted the North in such a positive light that they supposedly inspired some 200 southern blacks to move there themselves. Black churches also disseminated migrants' success stories. During church services, letters often were read aloud and discussed by the parishioners.

Some churches founded migration clubs. Members shared information about the North and how to get there. Club leaders wrote to northern businesses or employment agencies to find work for their members. One letter, from a migration club in Mobile, Alabama, read, "We have a club of 108 good men wants work we are willing to go north or west but we are not able to pay rail road fare now if you can help us get work and get to it please answer at once. Hope to hear from you."[6]

DECIDING TO LEAVE

Even with encouraging letters from friends and kin, making the decision to leave the South was difficult. People had to ask themselves many hard questions. Is living in the South really so bad? Is there no hope of improving my life here? Can I truly believe all the good news about the North? What if I make the journey and cannot find a job or a place to live? What will happen to relatives I leave behind in the South? Given all these considerations, the decision to move to the North was rarely a casual one. Instead, it was usually made after much thought and deliberation.

After people decided to make the journey, they then had to develop a strategy for how best to do it. Money was the foremost concern. Traveling to the North was fairly expensive. As the role of labor agents diminished, would-be migrants could no longer count on northern businesses to pay their way. They had to come up with the money themselves.

Some sold everything they owned—from land to furniture to clothes—to make the price of a train ticket. Others borrowed from family and friends. Families often pooled their money to send one member, usually a young man. He was expected to mail money home to help the rest of the family follow him. Frequently, a young couple decided to leave their children behind with the children's grandparents. Once the father and mother had established themselves, they would make plans to bring their children north.

Even using such strategies, some poorer African Americans still could not afford to take a single journey north. They had to make the trip in steps, often on foot or in a horse-drawn cart.

These migrants might move a short distance to a town or city and then work there until they could afford to make another short move. It could take years for these migrants to reach their final destination in a northern city.

For migrants who were able to make the trip in one step, the journey was still often difficult. The most fortunate took a train, although for an African American, train travel was far from comfortable. At least while they were still in the South, they had to sit in segregated waiting rooms and train cars, which usually were overcrowded and dirty. Traveling by bus or car held other challenges. Many restaurants and hotels would not serve blacks. The migrants could not be sure whether they could get food on the road or find shelter for the night.

WHO WERE THE MIGRANTS?

The Great Migration began with the American industrial expansion during World War I. But it continued long after the war ended in 1918. Throughout the 1920s, migrants continued to head north at a steady rate.

The migrants were a varied group. They were men and women, well-off and poor, young and old, rural and urban. However, there are some generalizations that can be made about the African Americans who chose to journey north.

The majority of migrants were fairly healthy and in their prime working years. They usually were ambitious people with enough of a sense of adventure to be excited by the prospect of starting over in an unfamiliar place. Initially, more men went north than women, but by the 1920s, more women began to travel to the North.

When the Great Migration began, most of the migrants came from the northernmost southern states, such as Virginia and Kentucky, largely because the trip was shorter for residents of these states. Over time, though, more and more migrants came from states farther to the south, especially Mississippi, Alabama, Georgia, and Texas.

Blacks who left the South were encouraged by stories of opportunities in the North told by the black press, recounted in letters from family and friends, and touted by labor agents and northern business managers. Hundreds of thousands of migrants sold all they had: land, household goods, clothes, anything that could be translated into cash. These emigrants created the first large, urban black communities in the North.

FACING THE CHALLENGE

During the Great Migration, the average migrant was thought to be an impoverished sharecropper who had to leave the South in order to survive. Later research has revealed that more than half the migrants came from southern towns and cities. They already were accustomed to urban living, which probably made the idea of living in a northern city less daunting than it would be to southern blacks who still made their living off the land.

The migrants also were somewhat more educated than the average African American in the South. A small percentage of them were skilled professionals, such as lawyers, teachers, social workers, and writers. These elites were eager to leave the South because the social climate made it nearly impossible for them to build thriving careers there. Some migrants were students who had studied at southern black colleges and who wanted to continue their education. Because the South lacked graduate schools that would admit African Americans, they had little choice but to head north.

No matter what their background, the African Americans who participated in the Great Migration were driven by the same need—to gain more control over their lives and their destinies. For a few, life in the North proved to be everything they dreamed it could be. But for many more, the experience was mixed. The North, they found, offered its own challenges—challenges that were different from those they faced in the South but that were, in some ways, just as difficult for them to meet.

Making
Their Way

In the autumn of 1921, a 19-year-old African American named Langston Hughes traveled to New York City to attend Columbia University. As he later wrote in his autobiography, *The Big Sea*, Hughes was not terribly excited about his future studies: "I really did not want to go to college at all. I didn't want to do anything but live in Harlem, get a job and work there."[1] Harlem, New York's biggest black neighborhood, was the destination of many participants in the Great Migration. By the time Hughes reached New York, these migrants had made Harlem the most famous African-American community in the world—a place that an ambitious and talented young black man like Hughes would naturally want to be a part of.

Many years later, he vividly recalled the excitement of seeing Harlem for the first time:

I can never put on paper the thrill of that underground ride to Harlem. I had never been in a subway before and it fascinated me—the noise, the speed, the green lights ahead. At every station I kept watching for the sign: 135TH STREET. When I saw it, I held my breath. I came out onto the platform with two heavy bags and looked around. It was still early morning and people were going to work. Hundreds of colored people! I wanted to shake hands with them, speak to them.[2]

Hughes eventually dropped out of Columbia and left the United States for some youthful adventures in Europe and Africa. But he remained enthralled with Harlem. He finally returned in 1929 and lived there for the rest of his life. Hughes, in fact, became one of Harlem's best-known residents. A leader in its burgeoning literary scene, he emerged as a great poet and novelist, whose work chronicled the struggles and joys of African Americans in the early twentieth century.

Hughes had an exceptional life, but he did have one thing in common with the more than one million other blacks arriving in a northern urban center during the Great Migration: the thrilling feeling of seeing a thriving black urban center for the first time. Some came to New York's Harlem, others to Chicago's South Side, and still others to Detroit's Paradise Valley or any of a number of other vibrant black communities in northern American cities. But all knew the same feeling of hope and fear, of excitement and uncertainty that accompanied their first glance at their new home in the North.

HELP FOR NEW MIGRANTS

At the height of the Great Migration, most migrants had a plan for what to do when they reached their destination. Many had friends or relatives who had previously settled there. The newcomers could rely on these earlier migrants to find them a job or give them at least a temporary place to stay. Even if migrants

Following World War I, more socially conscious and better-educated blacks settled in Harlem, creating a political and cultural center for black America. At the same time, a growing black middle class that advocated racial equality and black pride arose. A new generation of young writers and artists like Langston Hughes *(above)* took ownership of a movement called the Harlem Renaissance, giving a voice to the African-American experience.

did not personally know someone in the city, they likely had the name and address of a friend of a friend who could help them settle in.

Migrants also could rely on African-American service organizations such as the National Urban League in New York and the Chicago Urban League in Chicago. Through these groups, many thousands of migrants found jobs and apartments and obtained free clothing appropriate for northern winters.

Many migrants also were welcomed by business owners. When the migration began, some white employers were afraid to hire blacks based on racist stereotypes that blacks were unintelligent and lazy. But employers quickly learned that most migrants were hardworking and driven to succeed. The Ford Motor Company, for instance, cautiously hired 600 African-American factory laborers in 1910. Impressed by their work, Ford continued to hire blacks. By 1929, it employed approximately 25,000 African-American auto workers, who made up about one-quarter of its total workforce. Black laborers soon dominated several important industries, such as mining iron and manufacturing steel.

FINDING JOBS

It was hardly surprising that black migrants wanted to make the most of their employment opportunities in the North. After all, that was one of the main reasons they had left their southern homeland. Many African Americans worked long hours, often at more than one job. One migrant who worked in a foundry explained to the Chicago Race Commission why he worked so hard:

> I can quit any time I want to, but the longer I work the more money it is for me, so I usually work eight or nine hours a day. I am planning to educate my girl with the best of them, buy a home before I'm too old, and make life comfortable for my family.[3]

Some migrants also needed to earn money to help relatives back in the South. They may have taken money from kin for the journey north with the promise that they would send cash home once they found work.

Despite their determination, black workers often encountered problems in the workplace. Some businesses or trades continued to bar African Americans. Labor unions also generally refused to admit blacks. Employers sometimes took advantage of the situation by hiring African Americans to replace striking white union members. As a result, many whites resented the presence of black workers and accused them of stealing their jobs and lowering their wages.

Migrants also were frequently dissatisfied by the pay they earned. Some workers signed contracts with labor agents that fixed their wages at a certain level. In the South, the wage offered had sounded generous. But in the North, these workers found that, with a much higher cost of living, the money they were earning was far too little. Although wages varied from place to place and from industry to industry, most migrants felt the pinch of rising prices for food and other necessities.

LIFE IN BLACK NEIGHBORHOODS

High rents were especially troublesome. As more and more African Americans crowded into northern cities, they were forced out of areas where whites lived and into all-black neighborhoods. Blacks who attempted to buy homes in white neighborhoods risked becoming a target of violence from whites. In one notorious instance, an African-American physician named Ossian Sweet was confronted by an angry mob when he dared to move into a white area of Detroit in 1925. Armed with shotguns, he and several friends holed up in the house. At one point, they shot into the advancing crowd, killing one man and injuring another. In a highly publicized court case, Sweet was tried for murder, but, by arguing that the shootings were in self-defense, he was acquitted.

The numbers of people moving north increased so significantly among blacks that there were housing shortages. People found themselves competing for even the most run-down housing, which went for higher rents than other areas. In 1928, the Harlem Tenant League held protests against the state legislature, claiming that blacks were segregated in Harlem and made "the special prey of rent gougers."

Black neighborhoods often were in the oldest, most dilapidated parts of town. There also were not enough dwellings to comfortably house all the new residents. Landlords divided apartments into smaller and smaller units, many of which had no bathrooms or kitchens. With demand for housing on the rise, landlords also were able to charge high rents. In the 1920s, Harlem apartments cost an average of 20 percent more than comparable apartments in other parts of New York City.

Disease spread quickly through overcrowded black areas. The residents often fell prey to outbreaks of pneumonia, tuberculosis, and smallpox. These health crises were worsened by a shortage of city hospitals that would treat African Americans. Adding to the misery of living in black slums, police often harassed their residents. Large numbers of blacks were arrested and imprisoned on minor, often trumped-up charges. Newspapers reported on the high rate of crime among recently arrived immigrants, which fueled whites' uneasiness with the tide of African-American immigration.

THE RED SUMMER OF 1919

During the summer of 1919, the whites' fear of blacks erupted into violence. World War I, which the United States had entered in 1917, had ended the year before. American soldiers returning home were surprised by the influx of African Americans into northern cities. Many white soldiers were upset to find themselves competing with recent migrants for jobs.

These racial tensions led to dozens of race riots during what African-American author and activist James Weldon Johnson dubbed the Red Summer of 1919. The worst violence occurred in Chicago. There, on a hot July day, a boy named Eugene William was floating in the water off the city's 28th Street Beach. By custom, the beach was divided into portions for whites only and blacks only. When William accidentally crossed into the whites-only area, an outraged white swimmer

(continues on page 48)

"I'D LIKE TO SHOW YOU HARLEM!"

On April 2, 1921, the magazine *The Independent* published a glowing description of Harlem, which, with the immigration of African Americans from the South, had become one of the largest black neighborhoods in the country. "I'd Like to Show You Harlem!" was written by Rollin Lynde Hartt, a white journalist and minister. Writing for a white readership, Hartt portrays Harlem as vibrant and prosperous, but he ends his piece by alluding to the race riots of 1919 and speculating about the possibilities of future racial "trouble."

> Greatest negro city in the world, [Harlem] boasts magnificent negro churches, luxurious negro apartment houses, vast negro wealth, and a negro population of 130,000, or possibly 150,000, or, as enthusiasts declare, 195,000. Only fifteen years ago Harlem was white. Today it is an exhibit, not of darkest, but of brightest Africa. . . . A negro said to me once, "There's no finer section of New York City."
>
> It was not a particularly wild exaggeration, you will find.
>
> True, a certain amount of poverty and a certain very pitiable degree of overcrowding occasionally lurk behind those brownstone fronts or sadden the interiors of less antiquated dwellings, and one hears on official authority that crime and illiteracy in Harlem are above "normal." Yet what meets the eye is all but universally cheerful—streets broad and well kept, houses scrupulously cared for, and the inhabitants admirably prosperous. . . . You see expensively clad mothers perambulating superb baby carriages. Beside Little Italy and the Ghetto, Harlem shines. And if its people are black, who cares? In ten minutes or less, you begin to forget, and in a half-hour or less you are color-blind, quite. . . .
>
> [N]egroes have gone into business—the real estate business, the insurance business, the amusement business, and a dozen other kinds of business, large and small. A negro millinery

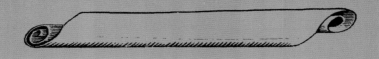

[hat making] shop offers "a variety of styles in the latest Parisian shapes" created "by expert negro designers." A negro apothecary advertizes, "Why Not Go to Our Own Drugstore? They employ all colored men." . . . Young Harlem will soon be independent of "the other race." . . .

Harlem reads enormously. . . . [It] supports five negro news-papers, all of which endeavor persistently—and successfully—to keep race problems uppermost in Harlem's mind. One result is a growth of race pride. . . . [S]ignificant is the thriving trade in negro doll-babies. You find them displayed everywhere, with the legend, "Why should a negro child play with a white doll?" . . .

[L]ittle by little, black Harlem is spreading. Is it not conceiv-able, then, that somewhere along its borders, if not within it, there may develop the spirit that leads eventually to race warfare? Today, by all one can learn, no such spirit exists, tho Harlem is on its guard against just that sort of thing, and whenever the white race wants "trouble," "trouble" will be forthcoming. There are "guns."

I have this from inside. During the series of race riots, in Chicago, Washington, and elsewhere—not so long ago it was—a police officer consulted a leading negro in Harlem. "How's this?" said the officer. "Coming up the subway stairs, I notice that every negro's hip pocket bulges out, and I feel, and, sure enough, there's a gun. What would you advise me to do? Enforce the law against carrying concealed weapons?"

"My advice is, let 'em alone. They won't start anything. But if somebody else does, taking away all the guns you can won't make any difference. There'll be thousands more."

So the officer did nothing. And Harlem did likewise.*

---

*Steven A. Reich, ed., "Primary Documents," *Encyclopedia of the Great Black Migration*. Santa Barbara, Calif.: Greenwood Press, 2006.

(continued from page 45)
pummeled the boy with rocks until he drowned. African-American witnesses told a white policeman who threw the rocks, but he refused to do anything. The witnesses then attacked the policeman, setting off five days of violence that rocked the city's South Side. Before the riot ended, 23 blacks were dead, more than 500 were wounded, and some 1,000 were left homeless.

OLD RESIDENTS AND NEWCOMERS

Recent migrants faced hostility not just from their white neighbors but also from blacks who had long made their home in the North. Many northern blacks were disturbed by the large number of southern blacks moving into their neighborhoods. They rightly feared that racial relations would suffer because of the Great Migration. For the most part, urban whites had learned to coexist in relative peace with the small groups of African Americans living within their cities. As more blacks came north, however, that delicate social balance was disrupted, and whites began to lash out not just at newly arrived migrants but also at longtime black city dwellers.

Some northern blacks also blamed the newcomers for their deteriorating neighborhoods, rising rents, and decreasing wages. The reason for these problems, though, was not the migration of southern blacks but instead was the white reaction to it. Urban whites were responsible for restricting the housing available to blacks, which had the effect of segregating African Americans into high-priced slums. White employers, by discriminating against black workers, were responsible for limiting the jobs African Americans could hold and the pay they could earn.

Some northern blacks looked down on southern African Americans as their social inferiors. They scoffed at their "country" manners and mocked their lack of education. In fact, this stereotype of the backward southerner was far from fair. The migrants of the Great Migration generally were about as well educated as northern blacks. Some also were skilled professionals and tradesmen, who soon moved their way into the growing black middle class in the North.

Over time, these tensions within black urban communities began to fade. Migrants were quickly integrated into their new surroundings. Teachers, ministers, and newspaper reporters took it upon themselves to train the newcomers in northern customs and manners. At the same time, northern African Americans began to embrace elements of southern culture that the migrants brought with them from their homeland. Baptist churches, which were far more plentiful in the South, started popping up in cities in the North. Northern blacks embraced new music and dances introduced to them by migrants. Traditional southern foods became just as popular in the North. Even southern accents became a normal, accepted part of northern African-American life. This blending of northern and southern ways not only helped unify black urban communities, but it also helped make them into dynamic environments where new ideas could flourish.

Building Communities

As African-American migrants began to adjust to their new surroundings, they quickly changed the landscape of the urban North. The meshing of northern and southern black ways reshaped older black neighborhoods into something new and exciting. These vibrant communities were intriguing not only to African Americans; many whites in America and abroad were fascinated by the art, music, and customs that came to define urban African-American culture.

THE HARLEM RENAISSANCE

In many northern cities, African-American musicians, writers, painters, and intellectuals developed rich social and cultural scenes. The most famous group of black artists was the one associated with the Harlem Renaissance, an artistic movement that flourished in the 1920s and early 1930s. In addition to

Langston Hughes, the movement included such luminaries as poets Claude McKay and Countee Cullen, novelists Jean Toomer and Zora Neale Hurston, and actor Paul Robeson. Experimenting with modern forms of expression, the artists of the Harlem Renaissance sought to explore and represent the African-American experience in their work. They also promoted a sense of pride in the black community and gave voice to the desire of blacks at last to achieve equality within American society.

The works of Harlem Renaissance writers appeared in black-owned publications such as *The Crisis* and *Opportunity*, as well as in progressive national magazines including *The New Republic* and *The Nation*. Despite their high profiles, these authors were little known outside their own elite circles. Hughes once noted the movement's irrelevance to most working-class African Americans: "The ordinary Negro hadn't heard of the Harlem Renaissance. And if they had, it hadn't raised their wages any."[1] The Harlem Renaissance, however, did have influence in American literary and artistic circles by shining a spotlight on African-American creativity and artistic talent. Many of the participants in the Harlem Renaissance also traveled south to take teaching posts at black colleges. In this way, they helped to disseminate new ideas about African-American life that had been percolating in northern cities.

JAZZ AND THE BLUES

During the Great Migration era, African-American musicians had just as much, if not more, influence over American culture. As the first great rush of migrants arrived, northerners already were familiar with jazz, a musical style pioneered by southern African Americans. The jazz they heard, however, was played by white musicians, who had appropriated the African-American musical style. The migration brought many African-American musicians north. Jazz clubs quickly sprouted up in northern cities, where audiences could, for the first time, hear jazz performed by people who had originated the music.

Musicians could make a modest living in clubs in southern cities such as Atlanta, Georgia; New Orleans, Louisiana; and Memphis, Tennessee. But they all wanted to work in northern clubs, where they could make more money and earn the respect

BESSIE SMITH
(1894–1937)

Empress of the Blues

Popularly known as the "Empress of the Blues," singing star Bessie Smith was instrumental in building a national audience for Southern African-American musical styles during the Great Migration. Smith was born in Chattanooga, Tennessee, on April 15, 1894 (although she gave various birth years throughout her life). The youngest in a family of seven, she worked hard to raise herself out of poverty. As a young girl, she began her career as a street performer in downtown Chattanooga. During her teenage years, Smith played in a variety of traveling shows. Working as a chorus girl, she was befriended by Gertrude "Ma" Rainey, who also became a popular singing sensation.

Performing in her own shows, Smith left the South to tour northern cities such as Chicago, Illinois; Baltimore, Maryland; and Indianapolis, Indiana. There, her audiences were largely made up of southern African Americans who had recently migrated to the North. They enjoyed Smith's slow, earthy interpretation of the blues. The singing style, with its origins in the South, reminded recent migrants of home. Smith also sang songs that touched on familiar troubles. Her blues songs dealt with the trials of urban life, the difficulties of poverty, the horrors of domestic abuse, and the ever-present specter of racism.

of the best jazz musicians and most sophisticated fans. One such ambitious musician was trumpeter Louis Armstrong. In 1922, 21-year-old Armstrong left New Orleans to make his name in Chicago's jazz scene. Armstrong soon emerged as a star and is now regarded as one of the greatest musical geniuses of the twentieth century.

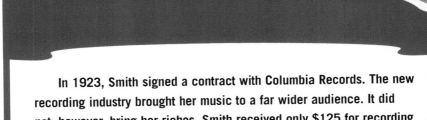

In 1923, Smith signed a contract with **Columbia Records**. The new recording industry brought her music to a far wider audience. It did not, however, bring her riches. Smith received only $125 for recording each side of her two-sided records. Her first recording, which featured "Down-Hearted Blues" on one side and "Gulf Coast Blues" on the other, sold an astonishing 780,000 copies in just six months, but she did not see a cent of its profits above her one-time flat fee.

Nevertheless, Smith became the highest paid African-American entertainer in the United States. The bulk of her income came from her live stage shows, which earned her up to $2,000 a week. The shows featured extravagant costumes and beautiful chorus girls, but Smith was always the main attraction. She was a large, tall woman who, with her flamboyant clothes and stage style, demanded attention. Smith was famous, too, for her onstage swagger and sexually suggestive lyrics. Offstage, she lived up to her rough and tough performing persona. Smith was notorious for her love of wild parties, heavy drinking, and numerous romances with both men and women.

During the Great Depression of the 1930s, Smith's popularity began to fade, but she continued touring until her career was tragically struck short. On September 26, 1937, she was traveling in a car when it hit a truck. Suffering massive internal injuries, Smith died in Clarksdale, Mississippi, at the age of 43.

The Cotton Club, one of the most famous nightclubs in the world, featured many of the greatest black entertainers of the era. In its heyday, the Cotton Club was the hot spot for both guests and performers. Ironically, it denied general admission to blacks and produced racist imagery in its shows.

Blues was another musical style that southern African Americans introduced to the North. Traditional blues songs spoke of the day-to-day struggles of rural blacks, but the blues appealed greatly to northern African Americans as well. After Okeh Records had success with "Crazy Blues" by singer Marnie Smith, record companies saw that there was a big market in selling recordings to African Americans. These recordings became known as race records.

African-American nightclubs in northern cities did more than introduce audiences to new, exciting talent. They also served as social centers for those new to the city. The nightclub scene gave newcomers a place where they could meet people and observe northern social customs. In addition, some clubs were rare venues where blacks and whites could mix socially. Bands also often included white musicians who wanted to learn how to play authentic jazz. The most famous nightspot of the 1920s, however, was the swanky Cotton Club. Although its entertainers were black, only whites were allowed to patronize this Harlem establishment.

BASEBALL, RADIO, AND MEDIA

The Great Migration fueled another form of entertainment—African-American baseball leagues. In the early twentieth century, black players were banned from professional baseball, which catered mostly to white fans. After large numbers of African Americans moved north, however, they created a concentrated black audience for the sport. In 1920, African-American pitcher Rube Foster established the Negro National League, which was made up mostly of teams in the Midwest. Two years later, several teams broke away and formed the Eastern Colored League. Promoted heavily by black-owned newspapers, the two baseball clubs were extremely popular in the 1920s. Star players were celebrities throughout black America.

In the late 1920s, the experiences of black migrants in the North became the subject of a nationally syndicated radio program, *Amos and Andy*. The hit show featured two white comedians playing black southerners who had recently moved to Harlem. With their inspiration coming from minstrel shows, the bumbling Amos and Andy were crude stereotypes. But as historian James N. Gregory points out in his book *The Southern Diaspora*, the radio program, which at its height had an audience of 40 million listeners, presented a varied portrait of black urban life. It included different types of African Americans—some naive and others knowing, some poor and others wealthy, some incompetent and others professional. With its layered depiction of Harlem society, the show, which stayed on the radio through the 1940s and made a brief appearance on television in the 1950s, was a favorite with blacks as well as whites.

Life among urban blacks also gained the attention of the national media. Magazines and articles were filled with descriptions of African-American neighborhoods, although the most ink was devoted to Harlem. In mainstream magazines such as *Harper's Weekly* and *The Saturday Evening Post*, readers could learn about Harlem's street life and nightspots. In the past, blacks in the media and popular culture usually were depicted as servants or field hands. Suddenly, because of the widespread curiosity about Harlem and its residents, African Americans appearing in popular culture more often were depicted as exotic and even glamorous.

RELIGIOUS BELIEFS

African Americans who participated in the Great Migration often felt uneasy with their new life in the North. It is hardly surprising that they turned to religion and churches for comfort. The earliest arrivals tended to join existing churches, some of which aggressively courted migrants to bolster their congregations. The Olivet Baptist Church in Chicago, for instance, actively sought out newcomers. It organized volunteer committees that provided migrants with a range of social services, including employment advice, housing placement, recreational programs, and child care. Committee members often met trains carrying migrants into the city so they could be the first people the newcomers would see when they set foot in Chicago. During the 1920s, Olivet's membership rose to about 9,000 parishioners.

The majority of southern blacks were Baptists, but in the North, African Americans had traditionally been Methodists. Many migrants did not care for Methodist churches, whose services generally were more sedate than those of southern Baptists. Instead of attending existing churches, a few migrants created their own, modeled on the churches they

During the Jim Crow era, many blacks refused to join white-led churches, where segregated seating arrangements and racist sermons were the norm. When blacks migrated north in large numbers, they assembled home-based and storefront churches that resembled those in their southern homes. In particular, storefront churches—places that reused small, empty stores in depressed areas where rents were low—were a crucial source of spiritual and social support for the influx of newcomers.

had known in the South. Some were modest endeavors run out of storefronts, but others grew large as they attracted more and more migrants.

Some newcomers lost interest in traditional churches. Already adventurous enough to take the trip north, they were willing to try a different type of religious experience, especially one that better filled their emotional needs. For example, tens of thousands of African Americans in New York joined the Kingdom and Peace Mission run by Father Divine. Divine's followers believed he was a living god. They were so devoted to him that they offered up their wages to Divine and worked for businesses operated by his church.

Several female religious figures also were embraced by migrant populations. Lucy Smith was a faith healer who became famous in Chicago and the surrounding area because of her dynamic preaching on the radio. Ida Robinson and Mother Rosa Horne founded large African-American churches in Philadelphia and New York City, respectively.

Although most urban African Americans remained Christians, a small minority adopted the tenets of Islam. Founded in 1913 by Noble Drew Ali, the Moorish Science Temple taught that blacks were descended from Muslims. Drawing loosely on traditional Islam, the religion became popular in several cities, but especially in Chicago. Even more influential was the Nation of Islam, which was founded in Detroit in 1930 by Wallace D. Fard. With its emphasis on African-American pride and unity, the Nation of Islam held a special appeal to migrants struggling to build a new life.

SEEKING POWER

Racial pride also was promoted by Marcus Garvey, a Jamaican-born activist who established the Universal Negro Improvement Association (UNIA) in 1916. Based in Harlem, Garvey held that African Americans needed to better their lives through self-respect and self-help. Deeply suspicious of whites, he urged blacks to separate themselves from the larger society. Garvey also wanted to create a new African homeland where all the blacks of the world could live in freedom. His message attracted a large following, particularly among poorer African Americans who had recently arrived in the North. It also disturbed whites frightened by the idea of an empowered black

Oscar Stanton DePriest, the son of former slaves, was a successful businessman and politician. In 1928, he became the first black congressman elected to the House of Representatives from a northern state. His election marked an era of black political organization in urban northern cities and was a source of pride for many. Some African Americans watched his first day in Congress from the segregated visitors' gallery.

population. The U.S. government eventually deported Garvey, and without his leadership, the UNIA fell into disarray.

Northern African Americans, however, continued to fight for greater power in American society. For many migrants, one of the greatest attractions of the North was that they would be able to vote. Unlike the South, the North offered them the chance to participate in the political process. Not surprisingly, these migrants were enthusiastic about getting involved in local politics.

During the Great Migration, white politicians in northern cities quickly realized the importance of the new voting bloc represented by recently transplanted blacks. They learned to tone down racist rhetoric so as not to alienate African-American voters. A few even began courting the votes of blacks. In Chicago, mayoral candidate William Hale Thompson actively campaigned in black neighborhoods. He promised residents more job opportunities and fair treatment from the city government.

Some black politicians also began to rise in city politics. Most were endorsed by and indebted to white politicians, but they still were able to wield a certain amount of power. The most successful was Oscar Stanton DePriest. With the support of Thompson, in 1915, DePriest became the first African American to serve on the Chicago City Council. In 1928, he made history by being elected to the U.S. House of Representatives. He was the first black person to serve in Congress since the end of Reconstruction. He was also the first African-American congressman from the North.

DePriest's rise was symbolic of how the Great Migration was changing not just the North, but the entire country. Throughout American history, African Americans had largely been a regional population, isolated in the South, where they were segregated from white society. Now, as their numbers were growing in the northern states, they were rapidly becoming a national population—one that was finally in a position to demand the acknowledgment, attention, and respect accorded to other citizens of the United States.

Depression
and War

During the 1930s, the world economy entered a depression. In the United States, some people lost their life savings after the price of stocks plummeted. Many more lost their jobs, as businesses and industries shut down or cut back in response to the severe economic downturn. The unemployment rate soared to 25 percent. Without jobs and without hope, millions of Americans were left hungry and homeless.

The Great Depression also marked the end of the Great Migration. Fewer African Americans in the South could afford the trip to the North. Life in the North also was far less attractive than it had been in previous years. As the economy worsened, southern blacks no longer could assume they would find employment in northern cities. In fact, even blacks who had migrated earlier had trouble getting work. Employers tended to lay off African-American workers first, leaving many jobless with few employment prospects. Some gave up and reluctantly moved back south, where at least they had friends and family to help them struggle through the hard times.

THE AGRICULTURAL ADJUSTMENT ACT

The economic conditions in the South, however, were no better. For farm workers they were especially grim. The South's agricultural economy still relied heavily on cotton. During the depression, already sagging cotton prices fell dramatically. Unable to earn a living from their crops, many farmers went bankrupt and lost their land.

The administration of President Franklin D. Roosevelt took action to relieve the plight of southern farmers. As part of its New Deal policies, which were designed to help Americans survive the Great Depression, the administration pushed for the passage of the Agricultural Adjustment Act in 1933. This law allowed the federal government to pay farmers to reduce the amount of land they cultivated. With smaller harvests, the demand for the crops farmers did grow would rise, which in turn would increase crop prices.

According to the act, farm owners were supposed to share a percentage of the payments they received from the government with any sharecroppers working their land. But in practice, few farm owners did. They often bullied sharecroppers into signing agreements to forfeit their share. Illiterate sharecroppers, unable to read the documents, had no idea what they were agreeing to. Other farm owners evicted their sharecroppers, only to hire them back as wageworkers. In this way, they could compel African Americans to work their farms without being legally obligated to give them a portion of their government payments.

Black and white sharecroppers banded together to protest these practices. They formed the Southern Tenant Farmers' Union in 1934 to demand their share of federal farm payments and to end the evictions. The labor union, however, failed to force any meaningful changes in Roosevelt's agricultural policies.

The Agricultural Adjustment Act also hurt sharecroppers because some farm owners used their federal payments to buy tractors, mechanized cotton pickers, and other farm equipment. Previously, they had not bothered to make such purchases because the cost of African-American labor was so cheap. But with lump sums of cash from the government, farm owners decided to go ahead and invest in labor-saving equipment. As a result, they needed fewer African Americans to work on their farms. Many former sharecroppers, forced to accept extremely low-paying wage work, now could not find any jobs at all.

For wealthy landowners, the Agricultural Adjustment Act was a boon. For African-American farm workers, it was a disaster. At the best of times, sharecroppers could barely eke out a living. But during the Great Depression, as the practice of sharecropping declined by half, many lost their livelihood altogether.

LOOKING TO THE NORTH

In the late 1930s, desperate southern blacks again began to seek out a better future in the North. Although the depression had not yet ended, industries that manufactured weapons, tanks, airplanes, ships, and other military supplies were looking for workers. Just as World War I had increased the market for military goods produced in the United States, a new European conflict—dubbed World War II (1939–1945)—revived the American manufacturing industry. The employment boom grew even bigger after December 1941, when the United States entered the war.

Southern industries produced some needed goods, such as textiles, oil, and steel. To take advantage of job opportunities in these businesses, many African Americans left rural areas and moved to southern towns and cities. But for large numbers of southern blacks, getting out of the South was just as important as getting a job. They were eager to head north to work because it still represented freedom from the segregation and discrimination they continued to face in the southern states.

During the Second Black Migration, an estimated 5 million blacks migrated to cities in the North, the Midwest, and the West. During World War II, people who could only find low-paying jobs in the South were able to get well-paying jobs in the defense industry and the shipyards. Because race discrimination was prohibited by law in the defense industry, many blacks and whites worked side by side.

Blacks in the South who had once lived in the North also were excited by the prospect of returning. The story of a factory worker named Charles Denby illustrates this strong desire. Originally from rural Alabama, he moved to Detroit to work in an auto plant in the early 1920s. "But I was laid off in 1929," he later explained, "and the little money I had saved was soon used up. . . . All winter I walked the streets." He went back to Alabama to weather the depression, but he had a hard time adjusting to the southern social system that required blacks to defer to whites. As Denby noted, "If you've been away they gave it to you even worse than if you stay. I told mother I'd rather be in prison in Detroit than to be free in the South. She cried and felt bad."[1] Denby unhappily remained in the South until 1943, when the wartime economy again allowed him to get work in Detroit.

FIGHTING FOR WARTIME JOBS

Despite labor shortages, many companies in defense industries initially refused to hire black workers. A. Philip Randolph, a noted African-American civil rights leader and labor organizer, decided to take action. In 1941, he began organizing a mass protest. He called on African Americans to participate in a march on Washington to force the Roosevelt administration to end racial discrimination in the wartime industrial build-up. Randolph claimed, "The administration leaders in Washington will never give the Negro justice until they see masses—ten, twenty, fifty thousand Negroes on the White House lawn!"[2]

Black-owned newspapers took up the cause. The *Chicago Defender* declared that 50,000 protestors were sure to join the march. The *Amsterdam News* was even more optimistic. It promised that no fewer than 100,000 African Americans would descend on Washington to make their voices heard.

In the end, however, there was no need to march. Randolph and Walter F. White, the secretary of the National Association for the Advancement of Colored People (NAACP), met with

Roosevelt on June 18, 1941. Fearing the embarrassment that a massive protest would bring to his administration, the president asked them simply, "What do you want me to do?"[3]

JACOB LAWRENCE
(1917–2000)

Painter of the Great Migration

One of the most influential African-American artists of the twentieth century, Jacob Lawrence used his talents to document the joys and sorrows of the first wave of black migration to the North. Lawrence was born in Atlantic City, New Jersey, on September 7, 1917. When he was 13, his family moved to Harlem in New York City. At the time, African Americans generally were not admitted into formal art schools. While in high school, however, Lawrence was able to take classes at the Harlem art workshops held at the public library on 135th Street (now the Schomburg Center for Research in Black Culture). There, he studied with African-American artist Charles Alston. Lawrence also frequently visited the Metropolitan Museum of Art to familiarize himself with the works of great modern masters. With Alston's help, Lawrence established a studio and met many of the leading African-American artists of the day, including poet Langston Hughes, novelist Ralph Ellison, and painter Romare Bearden.

In 1941, when Lawrence was only 23, he received a $1,500 grant from the Julius Rosenwald Fund to create a series of paintings. Lawrence chose as his subject the experiences of southern African Americans who had migrated to the North after World War I. He drew on stories he had heard from these migrants, including his parents. He also spent many days in the 135th Street library, poring over books about the Great Migration.

Lawrence called his series *The Migration of the Negro*. It included 60 paintings on panels of slate. With flat, stylized figures

The result was Executive Order 8802. This order banned all employment discrimination in industries receiving government defense contracts and in government offices on the basis

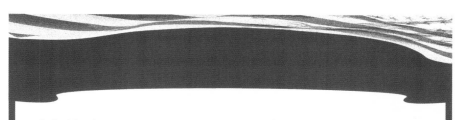

in bold primary colors, Lawrence communicated not just the physical journey but also the emotional one that took the migrants from the South to the North. Half of the paintings depicted the violence and poverty they had escaped, while the other half showed the new urban landscape they discovered. All the paintings had simple yet poetic captions, which artist Gwendolyn Knight helped Lawrence write. (Lawrence and Knight were married in 1941.) *The Migration of the Negro* was shown at Edith Halpert's Downtown Gallery and was featured in *Fortune* magazine, before being sent on a two-year tour as a traveling exhibition.

Lawrence's masterpiece was just the beginning of an extremely prolific career. He painted a wide variety of subjects dealing with African-American life and history, including portraits of historical figures such as Harriet Tubman and Frederick Douglass. Lawrence's personal experiences serving in World War II and being treated in a hospital for depression inspired additional series. Late in his career, Lawrence explored the worlds of construction workers and the buildings they made.

Lawrence's work appears in the collections of more than 200 museums, including the Metropolitan Museum and the Whitney Museum. His painting *The Builders* (1947) now hangs in the White House. Among the many honors Lawrence earned during his long career was the prestigious Spingarn Medal from the NAACP and election to the American Academy of Arts and Letters. Lawrence continued painting until his death on June 9, 2000, at the age of 82.

of race, nationality, and gender. Roosevelt's action did more than simply help African Americans gain access to wartime jobs. It also demonstrated what even the threat of a protest could do to secure their civil rights—a lesson that they would not soon forget.

HEADING WEST

The majority of factories producing military goods were located in the Northeast and Midwest. Many blacks looking for wartime work, therefore, traveled to the same cities as the participants in the Great Migration. But some manufacturing facilities important to the war effort were based in cities on the Pacific coast. They included airplane manufacturers such as Boeing and Lockheed and shipbuilders such as Kaiser and California Ship.

Unlike the earlier migrants, therefore, many black job seekers during World War II headed west. Most of them came from the westernmost southern states, especially Texas, Louisiana, and Arkansas. Their destinations included Los Angeles, Oakland, and San Diego in California; Portland in Oregon; and Seattle in Washington. There had long been a smattering of African Americans in the American West. For instance, about 2,000 blacks, including some slaves, went to California during the gold rush of the late 1840s and early 1850s. But the population of African Americans in the region ballooned during the war years. Between 1940 and 1945, the number of black Americans in the West rose from 171,000 to 620,000.

Moving west involved new challenges not experienced by earlier African-American migrants. For one thing, they had to travel a longer distance, often over rough terrain. Once they arrived, they felt further removed from the distant South and their relatives and friends there. In the West, too, they had to deal with their status as one minority population among many. Black newcomers had to learn to get along with not just white westerners, but also with Mexican Americans, Chinese

Americans, and Native Americans who were far more established in the region.

Not all African Americans in the West worked in wartime industries. Some were part of the military. About 14,000 African Americans were stationed at Fort Huachuca in Arizona. The base, home to the all-black 93rd Infantry Division, housed the largest group of African-American soldiers during World War II.

THE DETROIT RIOT OF 1943

In the war years, photographs of uniformed black sailors and soldiers were prominent in the black press. Articles trumpeted their courage and heroism. Even though the U.S. military remained segregated throughout the war, these images and stories conveyed a sense of optimism for the future. They suggested that the country would be grateful for the distinguished military service of African Americans and would perhaps soon grant all American blacks at home the respect they deserved.

Those hopes soured during the summer of 1943, when the rapid influx of blacks into manufacturing centers reignited violent racial hostilities like those last seen in 1919. In several cities—including Los Angeles, California; and Mobile, Alabama—race riots broke out. Detroit, Michigan, however, saw the worst violence. There, on June 20, 1943, an integrated crowd filled an amusement park on Belle Isle, an island off the coast of the city in the Detroit River. During the hot evening, a few minor fights broke out between black and white teenagers. But tensions escalated when African Americans tried to leave the island and reenter the city. On the other end of the bridge, they were attacked by thousands of whites.

The fighting quickly spread throughout Detroit. Wild rumors helped fuel the violence. Blacks said that white rioters had thrown an African-American woman and her child off the Belle Isle bridge. Whites said that an African-American man had raped and murdered a white woman there. On the second

With the passing of the Fair Employment Practices Act, which declared discrimination in employment to be against the law, thousands of blacks moved to Detroit to work in the defense industry. Tensions between blacks and whites came to a head on June 20, 1943, during an altercation that resulted in a three-day riot. Federal troops were finally called in to restore peace.

day of rioting, white mobs rushed into Paradise Valley, the slum area where most of Detroit's African-American population lived. The fighting continued until President Roosevelt sent 6,000 federal troops into the city to restore order. The troops occupied Detroit for the next six months.

The racial violence in Detroit and other American cities taught a painful lesson to the country's black citizens. Their labor—both in manufacturing and in the military—was helping the United States fight a war to liberate Europe from the armies of America's enemies. But in their own nation, they themselves still were not truly free.

The Second Wave

World War II ended in August 1945. However, the migration of southern blacks sparked by the war continued. In fact, this second wave of migration exceeded the first one. In the earlier Great Migration, which lasted roughly from 1915 to 1930, about 1.25 million African Americans came north. In what is sometimes called the Second Great Migration, which occurred from about 1940 to 1970, approximately 4.5 million blacks participated. By its end, one out of every seven African Americans originally from the South now lived in the North or the West.

Historians have long seen the Great Migration as a pivotal event in American history. But the Second Great Migration has received far less attention, even though the second wave involved three times as many people. The second migration was not only larger, but it also was more significant. In many ways, it created even more lasting changes in African-American life.

THE NEW MIGRANTS

Immediately after the war, the migration rate fell slightly, as wartime work dried up. But southerners continued to make the journey north steadily throughout the 1950s and 1960s. Many felt they had little choice. After 1950, the mechanization of southern agriculture left African-American farm workers with fewer jobs than ever. Large numbers of rural blacks had to move to southern cities to find work. Some decided that, if they had to uproot themselves, they might as well travel to the North, where they could also free themselves from the social constraints of segregation. Because of the migrations within the South and from the South to the North, by mid-century, for the first time in American history, more African Americans lived in urban areas than in rural areas.

In the post-war era, the majority of migrants came from five states of the Deep South: Alabama, Georgia, Louisiana, Mississippi, and South Carolina. As in the earlier Great Migration, those who participated varied in age, background, and experience. But many had certain characteristics in common. They tended to be younger and better educated than the average southern African American. They also frequently had experience with urban life. During the 1930s, many southern blacks moved to southern cities such as Atlanta, Georgia; Birmingham, Alabama; Memphis, Tennessee; and Houston, Texas. For them, the adjustment to northern and western cities was smoother than it was for migrants fresh off the farm.

In some respects, migrating was easier for people in the second wave. By the time they were heading north, moving anywhere in the United States had become less daunting than before. The federal highway system made car travel faster and more comfortable. More migrants also had access to moving vans, which allowed them to carry treasured possessions to their new homes.

Some African-American migrants to the Northeast and Midwest headed for smaller cities, including Toledo, Ohio; and Rochester, New York. Still, most continued to move to the same large cities—such as New York, New York; Chicago, Illinois; and Detroit, Michigan—that were popular during the Great Migration. By going there, they had the advantage of knowing what they would find at their destinations. Even with accounts of northern life in the black press and in letters from friends, some migrants during the Great Migration were ill-prepared for their new environment. They had to struggle to adjust not only to northern ways but also to city living. Later arrivals in the second wave, on the other hand, had a fairly good idea of the kinds of lives they would lead in the North. The massive press attention to Harlem and South Side Chicago made black Southerners very familiar with these neighborhoods long before they decided to head north.

The second wave of migrants also included more women than the first. During the war, as male workers were drafted into the military, defense industries began recruiting women for manufacturing work. For black women, these factory jobs were very attractive. In the past, most African-American women who came north could only find work as household servants. Being a factory worker paid much higher wages and, if the factory was unionized, also frequently offered generous benefits.

When the war ended, a new group of African Americans headed for the North and West—black veterans. Many had fought overseas. After returning home, they had little interest in settling down in the South. They were eager for the good jobs the North offered. It also was easier in the North to get an education through the GI Bill (1944), a federal law that provided funds to pay veterans' tuition.

THE POSTWAR JOB MARKET

At the end of the war, the decrease in defense work made the West much less attractive to most African Americans. In some cities, many recent black migrants were laid off from their lucrative manufacturing jobs, prompting some to leave the West altogether. For instance, the African-American population of Portland, Oregon, declined by 50 percent between 1944 and 1947.

African-American soldiers who had been stationed at western military bases were an exception. After the war, many black veterans already in the West found the area hospitable enough to stay. They were joined by a continuing small stream of southern migrants, although the rate of western migration never again reached its wartime peak.

Following the war, the labor market changed to suit a peacetime economy. African Americans had a harder time getting jobs in manufacturing, but they began to gain access to other types of well-paying work. In northern cities, blacks increasingly were hired by the local and federal government. Many found jobs as teachers, post-office employees, and office workers. Others worked in private firms as clerks and salespeople, although usually blacks were hired for these jobs only if the businesses' clientele was primarily African Americans.

DISCRIMINATION IN HOUSING

While job opportunities opened up, blacks still had problems finding housing in urban areas, especially in the tight housing market following the war. African Americans remained confined to certain neighborhoods. There, houses and apartments became more scarce and expensive as the second wave of migration continued.

Even African Americans who made a good living often were unable to buy houses because of the policies of the federal government. The Roosevelt administration had established the Federal Home Administration (FHA) to guarantee mortgages, which helped many Americans afford to buy houses. It was the job of the Home Owners' Loan Corporation to evaluate neighborhoods to determine which ones qualified for the federally backed loans. To instruct banks, the organization drew color-coded maps to designate which areas were most worthy of the best mortgage terms. It enclosed any neighbor-

TWO GENERATIONS IN THE NORTH

Born in Harlem in 1937, Claude Brown was the son of southerners who had come north during the Great Migration. Working hard to achieve their dreams, his parents left Brown and his siblings—Carole, Margie, and Pimp—to roam the city streets. There, Brown came to see that the promised land his parents had hoped to find was in fact a hard world full of violence, crimes, and drugs. By his early teens, Brown was a drug dealer, thief, and veteran of several reform schools. Frightened by the toll heroin was taking on his friends, he left Harlem when he was 18. Brown earned his high school diploma in night school and then continued his education at Howard University. While a student there, he began writing an autobiographical novel about his rough youth in Harlem during the 1940s and 1950s. The acclaimed book, *Manchild in the Promised Land* (1965), became a best seller with more than 4 million copies in print.

In *Manchild*, Brown described the gulf between the children of his generation and their parents. For a young man raised in the North, he was not only embarrassed by his parents' southern customs; he also feared that their experiences in the segregated South had left them ill-equipped to deal with the harsh realities of northern city life.

It seemed as though the folks, Mama and Dad, had never heard anything about Lincoln or the Emancipation Proclamation. They were going to bring the South up to Harlem with them. I knew they had had it with them all the time. Mama would be telling Carole and Margie about the root workers [practitioners of a form of African-American magic] down there, about somebody who had made a woman leave her husband, all kinds of nonsense like that.

hoods with black residents in red and refused to allow banks to offer federally backed mortgages there. This practice of redlining ensured that whites could get much better mortgage

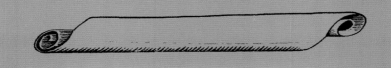

I wanted to say, "Mama, why don't you stop tellin' those girls all that crazy [s---]?" But I couldn't say anything, because they wouldn't believe me, and Mama figured she was right. It seemed as though Mama and Dad were never going to get out of the woods until we made them get out. . . .

I wanted to say, "Look, Mama, we're in New York. Stop all that foolishness."

She and Dad had been in New York since 1935. They were in New York, but it seemed like their minds were still down there in the South Carolina cotton fields. Pimp, Carole, and Margie had to suffer for it. . . .

I could understand Pimp's anxieties about having to listen to Grandpapa, who was now living with Mama and Dad, talk that old nonsense about how good it was on the chain gang. . . . I couldn't imagine them treating him nice, because I didn't know anybody in the South who was treated nice, let alone on a chain gang. Still, Papa said the chain gang was good. I wanted to smack him. If he weren't my grandfather, I would have. . . .

They didn't seem to be ready for urban life. . . .

They needed some help. The way I felt about it, I should have been their parents, because I had been out there on the streets, and I wasn't as far back in the woods as they were. I could have told them a whole lot of stuff that would have helped them, Mama and Dad and Papa, everybody, if they had only listened to me."*

---

* Claude Brown, *Manchild in the Promised Land*, New York, N.Y.: Touchstone, 1965, pp. 274–279

At the end of World War II, government policies favored suburban development, resulting in the middle and upper classes abandoning the cities for the suburbs. With them went tax money to build new infrastructure. The poor, many of whom were blacks who had migrated from the South in the 1920s and 1930s, faced declining property values, overcrowded and unsanitary conditions, and the elimination of some of the cities' public transport services.

terms than blacks and made it extremely difficult for African Americans to purchase homes.

Blacks also generally could not buy houses in white neighborhoods because of restrictive covenants. These were agreements that restricted homeowners from selling their property to African Americans. In 1948, the U.S. Supreme Court heard the case of *Shelley v. Kraemer*, which questioned the legality of restrictive covenants. The Court concluded they were unconstitutional.

Initially, however, the finding did little to break down the barriers to blacks wanting to move into white neighborhoods. Even someone as wealthy and famous as Willie Mays, a star baseball player with the San Francisco Giants, had difficulty purchasing a home in a non-black area. In 1957, Mays did succeed in buying the house he wanted, but only after the Giants's management and the mayor of San Francisco stepped in to help him. Mays's wife, Marguerite, spoke bitterly about their dealings with their white neighbors: "Down in Alabama where we come from, you know your place, and that's something, at least. But up here it's all a lot of camouflage. They grin in your face and then deceive you."[1]

WHITE FLIGHT

Despite white resistance, urban blacks continued to try to escape segregated ghettos and to move into traditionally white neighborhoods. These efforts resulted in what became known as "white flight." When a black family moved into a white area, many white neighbors left and resettled in suburban communities that were being built outside of city centers. The suburbs offered families newly constructed houses with large lawns that could be purchased with low-interest mortgages. But for many whites, moving to the suburbs was also a way to escape urban life.

Increasingly, whites viewed blacks and their urban communities with suspicion. These communities often were overcrowded, unsanitary, and unsafe. But white urbanites frequently exaggerated these conditions, especially the rates of crime and violence in black neighborhoods. For many whites of the 1950s and 1960s, it was largely fears of African Americans fueled by old prejudices that pushed them out of cities and into suburbs.

As suburbanization increased, many American cities began to follow a distinct pattern: Their core, called the "inner city," was populated by African Americans, while the surrounding suburbs were populated by whites. (The pattern is the reverse of what is found today in most cities around the world, where a city's wealthiest residents live at its center and its poorest residents live on the periphery.)

The "problem" of the inner city began to interest sociologists and other scholars. They examined the lives of urban blacks and, with little basis, concluded that African-American migrants were to blame for the deteriorating conditions of the neighborhoods. Many of these studies suggested that southern blacks had no ambition, were badly educated, and lacked a strong sense of family. These false claims were soon echoed in popular newspapers, magazines, literature, movies, and music. They generally portrayed black urban communities as places of such hopelessness, despair, desperation, and rage that they could erupt into violence at any second.

Probably the most famous fictional portrait of a damaged and doomed urban African American was the novel *Native Son*. Written by Richard Wright, it was the first national best seller by an African-American author. The book tells the story of Bigger Thomas, a young black man living in Chicago's South Side, who is so psychologically overwhelmed by poverty and racism that he becomes a murderer.

FIGHTING FOR EQUALITY

Many blacks living in cities, however, resisted the idea that their communities were some sort of national problem. They were well aware of the difficulties presented by high rates of unemployment, inadequate housing, and limited prospects. But to African Americans living in the inner city, their neighborhoods also were full of vitality and excitement. Building on the institutions established during the Great Migration, northern blacks and recently transplanted southern migrants worked together to create communities that helped their residents grow, thrive, and work for a better future.

The African-American press documented the latest news from these lively urban centers. Dozens of black-owned

In an effort to end racial segregation, young blacks took part in mass protests known as a sit-ins. The first sit-ins had little effect, but they soon strengthened throughout the country once civil rights organizations and wire services spread the word. Northern blacks and whites, who did not cope with the same segregation laws, also took part in these nonviolent and respectful protests. Above, a sit-in at Woolworth's in Atlanta in 1960.

newspapers emerged and flourished in this environment, although the *Chicago Defender* remained the largest and most influential newspaper in black America. Also in Chicago, magazine publisher John H. Johnson established a media empire. In 1942, he started publishing *Negro Digest*, a periodical modeled on *Reader's Digest* that collected articles for black readers. In

1945, Johnson launched *Ebony*, a large-format general interest magazine illustrated with photographs. Designed as a black version of the popular *Life* magazine, *Ebony* soon was selling hundreds of thousands of copies a month. And in 1951, Johnson's company began publishing *Jet*, a successful weekly news magazine geared to an African-American audience.

These publications, along with political monthlies such as the NAACP's magazine *The Crisis*, reported on the growing tide of activism among blacks in American cities. Concentrated into tight communities, urban blacks increasingly banded together to fight discrimination in the decades following World War II. They sought not only to integrate city neighborhoods but also to gain access to jobs, stores, and public spaces.

Civil rights groups, such as the Congress of Racial Equality (CORE), developed a variety of strategies for drawing attention to racial discrimination. Founded in 1942 in Chicago, CORE staged nonviolent protests against parks, swimming pools, restaurants, and other commercial businesses that refused to serve African-American patrons. One type of protest was the sit-in. During a sit-in, African-American activists gathered at an establishment that designated itself as for whites only. They then refused to leave until the police came to arrest them. The resulting publicity brought attention to their cause.

At the same time, the NAACP was trying to achieve racial equality through the courts. Some states still had non-discrimination laws on the books dating from the time of Reconstruction. Through lawsuits, the NAACP attempted to compel the authorities to enforce these laws, which long had been ignored. In *The Crisis*, the organization detailed its efforts and celebrated its victories to encourage other people and groups to try out similar strategies.

BLACK POLITICAL ACTIVISM

African-American activism also was encouraged by black urban churches. They provided free meeting places where people could come together and organize protests and rallies. But some churches played an even more active role in the escalating fight for civil rights. The church ministers, frequently officers in local chapters of the NAACP, sought to educate their congregations about political issues affecting African Americans and helped to recruit young people to work for social justice. Churches also helped to publicize events and raise funds for the activists' efforts.

One of the most politically involved northern churches was the New Bethel Baptist Church in Detroit. It was founded as little more than a prayer group in 1932 by migrants from Mississippi. The church grew rapidly after 1946, when the dynamic C. L. Franklin became its pastor. He urged his parishioners not only to support civil rights activism but also to become involved in the political process. Franklin's church organized voter registration drives and endorsed certain candidates based on their willingness to address issues of importance to African Americans. Franklin described the complex role he and other politically active ministers played in the postwar era:

> In Buffalo, or Detroit, or Chicago, or Los Angeles, the minister is involved. He helps his congregation in terms of presenting before them different candidates, and recommending. He leaves them free, of course, to choose; but he recommends certain people. . . . And the minister is interested in what the Board of Education is doing, if the classrooms are too crowded, things like that. He's involved in the total structure.[2]

In northern cities, African Americans gradually exercised more political influence. Their increased political awareness and involvement was only part of the reason. White flight also played a role. As whites fled to the suburbs, blacks became the majority population in some major cities. As a result, more

Blacks who attempted to register to vote faced possible beatings, arrests, shootings, and unpassable literacy tests. Despite this, black organizations such as CORE and the NAACP coordinated efforts to organize black voter registration campaigns and protest marches like this one led by Martin Luther King Jr and his wife, Coretta *(center, front)*, in Montgomery, Alabama, in 1965.

black mayors, state legislators, and even members of Congress won elections.

After the early 1930s, African Americans also became a force in the Democratic Party. Before that time, most black voters were Republicans, because the Republican Party endorsed the reforms of the Reconstruction era. But support for President Roosevelt, a Democrat, and his New Deal policies led African Americans increasingly to realign themselves with the Democrats. Over time, Democratic candidates running for office at all levels came to realize that they had to take the concerns of African-American voters seriously if they wanted to be elected.

The political influence of African-American voters and activists was evident in the passage of two important laws in the 1960s. The Civil Rights Act of 1964 ended racial segregation in schools, workplaces, and public facilities. The Voting Rights Act of 1965 outlawed practices designed to restrict African Americans' right to vote. These two laws were important to all African Americans, but they had a special meaning to those in the South. For the first time, southern African Americans finally could hope to enjoy basic civil rights without having to leave their homeland.

Heading Home

In the early 1970s, demographers—scientists who study changes in populations—noticed something strange. The rate of black migration from the South had started to slow during the 1950s, but by the late 1960s, the great stream of migrants had become little more than a trickle. Even more puzzling was the fact that, by 1970, there actually were more African Americans moving to southern states than moving out of them.

Throughout the 1970s and 1980s, the number of black migrants to the South grew steadily. But in the 1990s, it exploded. The movement was so large it began to look like a new migration, dubbed by some the Great Migration South.

This new migration trend was a surprise to social scientists. Most assumed that African Americans would continue to move from south to north as they had for much of the twentieth century. But they had failed to see that changing times compelled northern African Americans to rethink their relationship with the South. For many, strong social and political forces were pushing them from the North while at the same time pulling them toward the South.

DEINDUSTRIALIZATION

Both the Great Migration and the Second Great Migration began when foreign wars created a demand for goods produced by America's defense industries. Because these industries were based in the North (and, in the case of the second migration, in the West), southern blacks traveled to these areas confident that they could find jobs in manufacturing.

By the late 1960s, however, northern and western manufacturing jobs began to dry up. American companies had started relocating their factories to foreign countries, where the cost of labor was far cheaper than in the United States. Because of this trend, Detroit's auto industry—once a major source of well-paid union jobs for African Americans—went from employing 338,000 Americans in 1947 to just 153,000 in 1977.

The deindustrialization of the North and West made these areas far less attractive to southern blacks. Fewer were inclined to move to these regions, where the number of good jobs available seemed to drop more each year.

THE URBAN POOR

Poverty among urban blacks also was growing in the 1970s. In the previous decade, the federal government had attempted to help impoverished Americans through a series of programs called the Great Society. These programs provided special services including preschool education, job training, and food stamps that the poor could use to buy groceries. During the administration of President Richard Nixon in the early 1970s, however, many of these programs were cut or dismantled, adding to the desperation of unemployed and underemployed African Americans living in crowded, poor urban neighborhoods.

The auto industry provided a route to the middle class for blacks when other industries were unwilling to give them jobs. According to the *New York Times*, black autoworkers have been hit harder by the 2009 recession than other workers because they occupy jobs at all levels on the car production ladder, from plant workers to management to auto suppliers and car dealers. Above, the General Motors world headquarters sits near an abandoned building in Detroit.

Many of these people also lived in dilapidated and dangerous public housing. To relieve overcrowding in urban centers, in many American cities the government constructed housing projects for people with low income. By the 1970s and 1980s, the construction of these projects was seen as a disastrous mistake in city planning. Badly maintained and poorly policed, many became dens of drug abuse and gang activity.

RIOTING AND CRIME

In the late twentieth century, African-American enclaves within cities also were frequently racked with violence. One of the most disturbing instances was the Watts Riot of 1965. Already worn down by poverty and racial discrimination, the residents of Watts, a neighborhood in South Central Los Angeles, were angered by their mistreatment at the hands of white police-men. These emotions boiled over on August 11, 1965, when Los Angeles was experiencing a withering heat wave. A confrontation between a motorist and the police erupted into a full-scale riot. Ten thousand rioters took to the streets. More than 200 buildings and stores were burned and looted, and 34 people were killed. The riot left Watts in ruins.

Two years later, race riots rocked Newark, New Jersey, and Detroit, Michigan. Then in 1968, following the assassination of civil rights leader Martin Luther King Jr., cities throughout the United States saw mass violence. All of these events convinced Americans, both white and black, that northern and western cities were in crisis.

During this era, many African Americans who had left the South began to question their decision. Faced with high crime rates and racial violence, they started to feel that their new homes were just as dangerous as the South had been in the heyday of lynchings. Voicing the frustrations of many, Earnest Smith, a man who left rural Mississippi for Chicago in 1944, explained his disillusionment with the North in 1971: "For the first 20 years, life in Chicago was real nice. . . . But the last five years was when I come to gettin' scared. They killed King and the people started tearin' up the place. Crime in Chicago got so bad that I got scared and started carryin' a gun."[1]

THE SUNBELT

The old idea of the North as the Promised Land was fading. But at the same time, the idea of the South as a world where African Americans were condemned to a life of degradation was disappearing as well. To many blacks, the South instead started to look like the place that would give them the best chance of building a better life.

By the 1970s, as jobs were disappearing in the North, employment opportunities abounded in the Southeast and Southwest—a region that was nicknamed the Sunbelt. Instead of relocating their factories overseas, some Northern industrial firms headed south. The area offered them inexpensive land, a low cost of doing business, and often generous tax breaks from states eager to attract northern businesses.

The growth of private business was not the only thing that made the South attractive. The federal government also invested heavily in the area in the late twentieth century. With federal funds for building roads, airports, and transportation systems, the region once considered a backwater now seemed at the forefront of modern American innovation. The widespread use of air conditioning also made the South much more livable. The steamy heat of southern summers had been not only uncomfortable but also unhealthy because of the high rate of insect-borne diseases during the hottest months. With air conditioning, people could stay indoors when the heat was overwhelming, which allowed many businesses to function there year-round for the first time.

IMPROVING RACE RELATIONS

The civil rights movement had also had a profound effect on the American South. During the 1950s and 1960s, protests organized by King and other civil rights leaders had convinced the federal government to pass legislation, such as the Civil Rights Act and Voting Rights Act, that effectively dismantled Jim Crow. As legal segregation came to an end, the region became more appealing to blacks. Old prejudices remained, but as blacks and whites interacted more in schools, in neighborhoods, and in the workplace, prejudice grew less potent over time. Dick Molpus, the former secretary of state of Mississippi, described these changes: "It may be hard for people in other parts of the country to believe this, but if they look South they may see some beacons of hope in this nation. The Civil Rights Act totally transformed our state."[2]

Northern African Americans began reassessing the South as well. In the past, few former migrants ever thought about moving back there. But by the 1970s, the social progress in the region made some reconsider the idea. Interviewed by *Ebony* in 1971, Elijah Davis recounted why he was willing to return to Mississippi after spending 20 years in Indiana: "Before I left here years ago, there were places you couldn't go, places you couldn't eat at, and you couldn't make a decent living. But I can live in peace here. I can walk anywhere in town without fear."[3]

Disappointment with race relations in the North and West led some African Americans there to head south. Many migrants had expected to escape prejudice, only to discover that racism, although it was less obvious, was still widespread outside the southern states. Etta Willis, who left San Francisco and moved to a small town in Mississippi, explained to the *San Francisco Chronicle* in 1998 that she actually preferred the overt racism in the South to the coded version common in California:

> You don't have the racism here [in Mississippi] that you used to have; frankly I have experienced less racism here than I did in San Francisco. The racism in San Francisco is very hard to detect, but it's there. It's here too, but not like that. If someone doesn't care for you they tell you to your face, and I can't think of a time that's happened since I came back.[4]

FAMILY TIES

As conditions improved in the South, many former migrants returned in order to be closer to relatives. In many cases, they had moved north as young adults in the 1940s and 1950s. Now, decades later, they came back to help care for their elderly parents. In other instances, returnees were seeking the support of family members. Tired of living in poverty and discouraged by shrinking job opportunities, they headed south to live with relatives who could offer economic assistance or help with child care.

Still others returned to the South because it was a pleasant place to retire. For older people on fixed incomes, the region offered a lower cost of living, allowing their savings to go much further. By retiring in the South, they also found an escape from the frantic pace of big city life. Nancy Foster, who worked in the banking industry in New York City, retired to the suburbs of Charlotte, North Carolina, for just this reason: "I was

"WHERE MY ROOTS ARE"

Academy Award–winning actor Morgan Freeman was born in Memphis, Tennessee, in 1937, but he spent much of his youth in Mississippi. In the early 1960s, he left the South to pursue a career on the Broadway stage and in Hollywood films. He has since been hailed as one of the greatest American actors of his generation.

In 2004, an interview with Freeman appeared in *America Behind the Color Line: Dialogues with African Americans*. Titled "Home," the piece focused on Freeman's decision as an adult to return to Mississippi, where he spends most of his time when he is not working. Like many blacks who moved to the North or the West in the mid-twentieth century to advance their career, Freeman never lost the sense that his true home was in the South.

> People asked me when I went home to live, after becoming a major persona in theater, in film, good Lord, what is wrong with you? You can live anywhere in the world you want to. Why did you come here? And I said, because I can live anywhere in the world I want to, that's why. This is home. This is where my roots are. This is where my parents are buried. This is where I've always felt safest. . . .
>
> What's different for a black person about the South, in contrast to the North or the West of the United States, is that we built the South, and we know it. What I own in the South isn't because I went and bought it. What I own is my place here, because my

ready for a slower pace. I wanted to settle down and relax. I had never planned on coming back, but after so many hour-long commutes to work, you begin to place more importance on simplifying your life."[5]

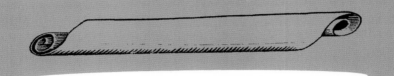

mother, my father, my grandmother, my grandfather, my great-grandmother, my great-grandfather, great-great-grandmother, great-great-grandfather, all the way back to my great-great-great-grandmother . . . that's where they had the farms. . . .

The South is the new comfort zone for blacks. . . .

Look at Atlanta. They're flooding into Atlanta. I said to my daughter, when she was going to college, where are you going to go to school, and she said, well, I don't know. I said, go to Atlanta; go to Spelman [College]. And when you get out of Spelman, you'll have a network. Well, she liked Spelman, and she's still in Atlanta. . . .

What we have always been blessed with is a sense of hospitality. And we have that for the simple reason that we're not overcrowded. There's room . . . [unlike] Chicago, San Francisco, any metropolis, any place where people are stuffed so close together. You won't get that here in the South. . . .

So I'll be buried here. My mother and father are buried right here, in front of the house. I've come back to my home place. Very few of us can go back to the home where we grew up. But those of us who can and do, I think will be very pleased in later years, when they sit on the front porch in a rocking chair, eat watermelon, fan the flies, and say, why did we give this up in the first place?*

* Henry Louis Gates, Jr., *America Behind the Color Line: Dialogues with African Americans*, New York, N.Y.: Warner Books, 2004, pp. 142–144.

Some participants in the new southern migration were children of people who had migrated north or west after World War II. Although they were born in the North, they still grew up with ties to the South. As children, many spent their summers there, living with grandparents or other relatives. The practice allowed children to get to know southern kin as well as escape from the threats of gang violence and the drug culture in their own urban neighborhoods. When these children became adults, they naturally considered starting careers in the South, where the job market was better. Unlike their parents, they had few memories of Jim Crow–era segregation. Instead of viewing the South as a hostile and dangerous world, they saw it as a welcoming place where they were surrounded by caring relations.

In addition to reuniting with family, some new migrants wanted to reconnect with their roots in the South. They considered the region their true home, even if they had spent many years in the North or West. In the South, these migrants saw the land of their ancestors, a place their forebears had loved even though they were enslaved. Poet Maya Angelou expressed these feelings in 1990 in an essay about why young African Americans were moving to the South in large numbers:

> [T]he American South sings a siren song to all Black Americans. The melody may be ignored, despised or ridiculed, but we all hear it. . . . They [migrants] return and find or make their places in the land of their foreparents. They find and make friends under the shade of trees their ancestors left decades earlier. Many find themselves happy, without being able to explain the emotion. I think it is simply that they feel generally important.[6]

THE NEW HARLEM

New black communities grew in the South as more African Americans moved there in the late twentieth century. These

Atlanta, Georgia, home to several prominent corporations including Coca Cola, UPS, Delta Airlines, and CNN, is one of the fastest-growing metropolitan areas in the country. The high rate of black migration and the large number of black professionals have supported the naming of Atlanta as "the black Mecca" or "a modern-day Harlem."

communities attracted still more newcomers, especially affluent blacks. Often, in the North, these wealthy migrants were the only African Americans in their upscale neighborhoods—a situation they sometimes found uncomfortable. In 2002, Renee Thomas explained to a television journalist her uneasiness with her old neighborhood in Philadelphia, Pennsylvania: "We were the first blacks that our neighbors' children had ever seen. You often feel like you don't fit in."[7] When she noticed her own son was uncomfortable around other African-American children, she decided to move to a largely black neighborhood in Atlanta, Georgia.

In 2005, about 50 percent of African Americans who moved to the South had a college education. They were lured both by companies that had established headquarters in the Sunbelt and by new, vibrant African-American communities in southern urban centers. Like Renee Thomas, many were drawn to the city of Atlanta. It became the most popular urban destination for migrants, attracting about three times as many as the second-ranking city, Dallas, Texas. Because of this flood of African Americans into Atlanta, Georgia welcomed more than twice the number of black migrants to any other state. Raymond Winbush, the director of the Race Relations Institute at Fisk University, explained Atlanta's appeal to African-American young adults: "Atlanta is to black America what Harlem was to black America during the great migrations earlier in the century. . . . Atlanta is perceived as a place of golden opportunity, with a culture in which African-Americans want to raise their kids—just the way California was 20 years ago."[8]

For much of the twentieth century, to African Americans, Harlem was far more than a neighborhood in New York. For those who did not live there, it was also an idea, an imagined place where blacks could find excitement, earn wealth, create art, raise families, build a better future, and enjoy freedoms that they had never known before. At the time, this imagined Harlem only could have been in the North. By the dawn of the twenty-first century, however, a "new Harlem"—Atlanta—had emerged deep in the heart of the South. This relocation of the African-American promised land from the North to the South marked an evolution in American race relations—one that was made possible by the millions of black migrants of earlier eras.

The Legacy
of the Great
Black Migrations

The twentieth century witnessed three waves of African-American migration. During the Great Migration (1915–1930), southern blacks moved to the Northeast and Midwest. During the Second Great Migration (1940–1970), they relocated to those areas as well as to the West. And during the ongoing Great Migration South, northern African Americans, including both southern-born former migrants and their northern-born children, reversed this trend by leaving the North and moving to the South.

The most obvious impact of these migrations was the effect they had on the migrants themselves. In each wave, the migrants had to leave their familiar surroundings and remake their lives in a new place—often a very alien environment where they had to learn new ways of speaking, dressing, and behaving. Even when participants knew a good deal about their destinations, the adjustments they had to make upon arriving still presented emotional and social challenges. The story of the African-American migrations since 1915, therefore, is one of courage and daring. Each migrant embarked on a quest into the unknown in search of something more, something better for themselves and their children.

The significance of these events, however, is more than just a collection of the personal migration stories. The migrations had a broader impact, touching on all Americans, whether or not they were migrants themselves.

SOUTH TO NORTH, RURAL TO URBAN

Before the twentieth century, 9 out of 10 African Americans lived in the South. As a result, black Americans were considered a regional population. Direct experience with African Americans, therefore, was largely unknown to many people in the rest of the country.

Because of the first two migrations, the so-called Black Belt—the large swath across the South where most African Americans were concentrated—all but disappeared. African Americans emerged as a national population, with a presence in every major city and in every state. As a result, the migrations allowed blacks to intermingle with whites and with other minority groups, which added greatly to the diversity of American society.

The migrations also transformed African Americans from a rural to an urban people. In the nineteenth century, agriculture already was becoming a less important part of the American economy. White Americans were increasingly leaving farms to work in city factories. But black Americans, largely confined to the South, remained in rural areas where it was becoming more and more difficult to make a living. Starting in the Great Migration era, they finally had the opportunity to work higher-paid jobs in manufacturing. Over the course of the twentieth century, as more blacks moved north and west for jobs in cities, they became just as urbanized as whites.

ART AND COMMERCE

In northern and western cities, African Americans were crowded into all-black neighborhoods. While this situation forced many people to live in substandard housing, it also compelled urban blacks to create new institutions and businesses. Without competition from white business owners, African-American entrepreneurs in black communities founded stores, banks, and other commercial establishments. As well as providing valuable services for their neighbors, successful businesses brought their owners more financial success than they could have hoped for in the South. Joining these businesspeople in the growing northern black middle class were better-paid factory workers and professionals such as doctors, lawyers, and teachers, who came north to pursue their educations.

The freedoms of the North not only allowed black entrepreneurs and professionals to thrive; they also gave black writers and artists a chance to practice their craft and find a broader audience. In turn, these opportunities gave creative works by African Americans more influence over American culture than ever before.

The intellectuals and artists of the Harlem Renaissance are well known today. But in their time, they had a relatively small audience among the black elite and among liberal whites. Even so, the Harlem Renaissance was an important movement because it made both blacks and whites take art and intellectual arguments made by African Americans seriously. It helped establish a multiracial audience for African American creative works, opening the door to such later greats as visual artists Roman Bearden, Jean-Michel Basquiat, and Kara Walker; and literary figures Richard Wright, Ralph Ellison, and Toni Morrison.

In popular culture, the migrants of the first two waves probably had their greatest influence in the field of music. From the

Richard T. Greene helped transform the Carver Federal Savings Bank in Harlem into the nation's largest black financial institution. He began his career as an executive assistant and worked his way up to the top as president.

beginning of the Great Migration, mixed-race urban audiences embraced jazz and the blues—musical styles that previously had been known largely only in the African-American South. Jazz has since been recognized as one of the most important American-born art forms. The blues has had an enormous influence over later popular musical styles, particularly rock and roll.

The years of the Great Migration also established African-American musical artists as culturally influential, not just for their music but for their personal style, fashion sense, and use of language. This trend continues today, with black hip-hop artists and rappers being embraced as style icons by Americans of all racial groups.

RELIGION AND POLITICS

The religion of southern blacks also had a big impact on the North. Before the twentieth-century migrations, the majority of people in northern cities practiced Catholicism, the religion of most European immigrants. African-American migrants, who were largely Baptists, helped spread Protestantism throughout the northern United States. The migrants' church services also tended to be livelier than those of northern Protestant sects. Therefore, they introduced to the North a new style of religion—one in which congregations were more vocal and in which spirited choirs played a more prominent role.

Northern churches also helped increase African Americans' political power. Prominent ministers endorsed candidates and used church services to educate congregations about political issues. This political involvement, of course, was possible only because southern migrants were able to vote in the North, a right denied them in their homeland. By moving north in large numbers, blacks were able to establish themselves as an important voting bloc, especially within the Democratic Party. In 1915, the majority of African Americans could not vote. Fifty years later, in 1965, black voters were a significant enough political force to push for the passage of the Voting Rights Act, which finally enfranchised African Americans in the South.

African-American voters have since used their influence on national, state, and local politics to elect black officials. Because of the Great Migration South of recent decades, African Americans increasingly held political office not just in the North and West, but in the South as well. Since 1965, black candidates have been elected mayor in dozens of major cities, including Los Angeles, New York, Philadelphia, San Francisco, Dallas, Atlanta, and Washington, D.C. Gains in black representation in Congress have been equally impressive. For instance,

(continues on page 104)

SHIRLEY FRANKLIN
(1945–   )

Mayor of Atlanta, Georgia

In January 2002, Shirley Franklin was sworn in as the mayor of Atlanta, Georgia. She was not only the first woman elected to head that city; she was also the first African-American woman ever to serve as the mayor of a major city in the American South.

Franklin was born Shirley Clarke on May 10, 1945, in Philadelphia, Pennsylvania. As a girl, she showed little interest in politics. Instead, she dreamed of becoming a professional dancer.

Shirley Franklin, the mayor of Atlanta, is the first African-American woman to serve a major southern city.

After graduating from Philadelphia High School for Girls, she attended Howard University in Washington, D.C. Studying sociology, Clarke earned a bachelor's degree from Howard and a master's degree from the University of Pennsylvania. While in college, she volunteered to work in the office of Shirley Chisholm, the first black woman to serve in the U.S. House of Representatives. Clarke became fascinated with how the political process could change citizens' lives for the better.

In 1972, Clarke married David McCoy Franklin. Like many African Americans of the 1970s, they decided that their future

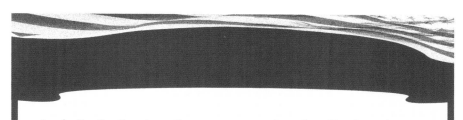

lay in the South, where the economy was booming. The Franklins moved to Atlanta. The city was a popular destination for the African Americans who participated in the Great Migration South, during which millions of northern blacks moved south. In Atlanta, the Franklins had three sons before they divorced in 1986.

Shirley Franklin became involved in city politics during the 1973 mayoral campaign of Maynard Jackson. She subsequently held a series of high-ranking jobs in Atlanta's government, including city manager. Franklin also was a member of the Atlanta Committee for the Olympic Games, which organized the Summer Olympics of 1996.

Despite her high profile in Atlanta, she had never run for elected office herself until 2000. Shy by nature, she decided it was time to overcome her fear of campaigning and run for mayor. For almost two years, she campaigned hard. Known for her personable manner and bleached-blond hair, Franklin slowly won over the voters. Although it was her first campaign, she managed to squeak out a modest victory.

Her first term in office was even more challenging than the campaign. Franklin discovered that the city was $82 million in debt. She had to push for unpopular measures, such as tax increases and layoffs of city employees, to balance the budget. Franklin also worked to restore voters' confidence in Atlanta's government, which had been notoriously corrupt during the previous regime. She asked the city council to pass legislation imposing a strict code of ethics on city employees.

Because of Franklin's tough governing style, *Time* magazine named her one of the five best big-city mayors in the United States. Franklin also won the Profiles in Courage Award from the John F. Kennedy Library Foundation in 2005. The same year, the voters of Atlanta reelected her with 90 percent of the vote.

(continues)

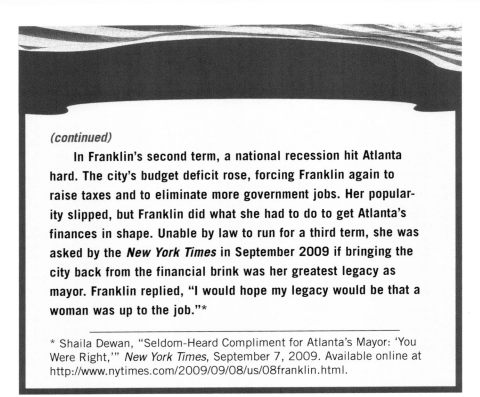

(continued)

In Franklin's second term, a national recession hit Atlanta hard. The city's budget deficit rose, forcing Franklin again to raise taxes and to eliminate more government jobs. Her popularity slipped, but Franklin did what she had to do to get Atlanta's finances in shape. Unable by law to run for a third term, she was asked by the *New York Times* in September 2009 if bringing the city back from the financial brink was her greatest legacy as mayor. Franklin replied, "I would hope my legacy would be that a woman was up to the job."*

---

* Shaila Dewan, "Seldom-Heard Compliment for Atlanta's Mayor: 'You Were Right,'" *New York Times*, September 7, 2009. Available online at http://www.nytimes.com/2009/09/08/us/08franklin.html.

(continued from page 101)

the 91st Congress (1969–1971) had 11 African-American members, while 40 years later, the 111th Congress (2009–2011) had 42, an increase of about 380 percent. Of these representatives, 16 were from southern states. As African-American politicians proved themselves in office, white voters became more comfortable with black candidates. As a result, Barack Obama was able to attract enough black and white supporters to win the presidency in 2008.

THE FIGHT FOR CIVIL RIGHTS

The great strides African Americans have made in the political culture and in American society at large are due greatly to the civil rights movement of the 1950s and 1960s. Although the movement was centered in the South, it had its roots in the North. Indeed, one of the most significant legacies of the African-American migrations north was the role northern black activists, including many migrants, had in inspiring the civil rights movement.

In the mid-twentieth century, African Americans in the North developed new ways to fight for equal access to good jobs, decent housing, and quality education. They boycotted stores that would not hire black workers. They staged sit-ins in public facilities that banned African Americans. And they took to the street and protested against institutional racism.

The actions of northern African-American activists were well known in the South. Southerners learned about them from friends and relatives who had migrated north, from northern black leaders and educators who visited the South, and most of all from black-owned newspapers and magazines largely based in New York and Chicago. These publications acted virtually as protest manuals for civil rights workers who later demanded that southern blacks be granted the same freedoms that northern blacks had fought for.

A NATION OF MIGRANTS

Americans have always liked to see themselves as pioneers and risk takers. They have long celebrated their forebears for shedding their past lives and looking to a new future, usually to the West, where they could build farms, dig for gold, or look for adventure in an uncharted land. This historical willingness to seek out a better, freer place to live remains an important part of the American character.

For much of the nation's history, however, African Americans were largely excluded from the migration stories that form the core of America's mythic self. First, they were literally enslaved. Then, they were confined in the hostile South by poverty and racism.

Only in the twentieth century were black Americans able to take charge of their own destinies, which often meant migrating to an imagined promised land. Like most other American migrants throughout history, their new home did not always live up to their highest hopes. But with time and energy and passion, African-American migrants succeeded in reshaping not only the land they moved to, but also the land they left behind, thereby transforming their lives, their society, and their nation.

Chronology

1879	Thousands of African-American "Exodusters" leave the South and migrate to Kansas.
1896	The U.S. Supreme Court finds that racial segregation does not violate the Constitution in its ruling in *Plessy v. Ferguson.*
1905	The *Chicago Defender,* a newspaper that will heavily promote the Great Migration, is founded.
1909	The National Association for the Advancement of Colored People (NAACP) is established.
1915–1930	Approximately 1.25 million southern African Americans head to the North during the Great Migration.
1916	The Pennsylvania Railroad Company sends thousands of southern blacks north to work on rail lines, initiating the widespread recruitment of African-American laborers by northern companies.
1919	Race riots break out in dozens of American cities during "Red Summer."
1920s–early 1930s	Black literary figures, artists, and intellectuals join the creative movement known as the Harlem Renaissance.
1928	Oscar Stanton DePriest becomes the first African American from the North to be elected to the U.S. Congress.
1930s	The Great Depression ends the Great Migration as southern blacks are no longer able to find jobs in the North.
1933	The passage of the Agricultural Adjustment Act contributes to the end of sharecropping, leaving

many rural southern blacks with no means of making a living.

1939   World War II breaks out in Europe, increasing the demand for products made by the American defense industries.

1940–1970   About 4.5 million African Americans move from the South to the North and West during the Second Great Migration.

1941   African-American civil rights workers persuade President Franklin D. Roosevelt to issue Executive Order 8802, which bans employment discrimination by race in industries receiving government defense contracts.

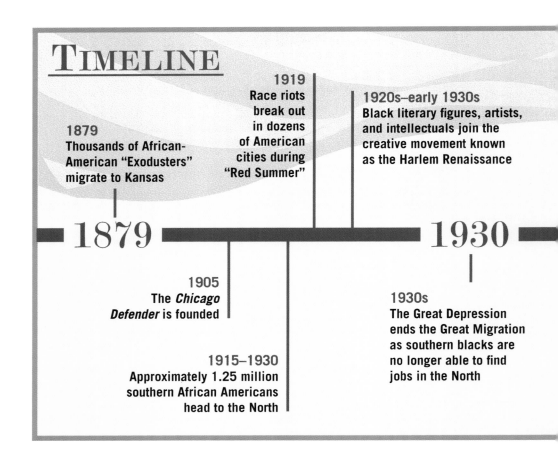

TIMELINE

1879
Thousands of African-American "Exodusters" migrate to Kansas

1919
Race riots break out in dozens of American cities during "Red Summer"

1920s–early 1930s
Black literary figures, artists, and intellectuals join the creative movement known as the Harlem Renaissance

1879   1930

1905
The *Chicago Defender* is founded

1915–1930
Approximately 1.25 million southern African Americans head to the North

1930s
The Great Depression ends the Great Migration as southern blacks are no longer able to find jobs in the North

1943   Federal troops take control of Detroit, Michigan, after the city is rocked by a massive race riot.

1945   John H. Johnson begins publishing *Ebony*, a popular general interest magazine for an African-American audience.

1948   The U.S. Supreme Court rules that restrictive covenants are unconstitutional, which allows more blacks to buy houses in white neighborhoods.

1954   In *Brown v. Board of Education*, the U.S. Supreme Court finds that segregation in public schools is unconstitutional, which accelerates the flight of white city residents to the suburbs.

1940–1970
About 4.5 million African Americans move from the South to the North and West during the Second Great Migration

1954
In *Brown v. Board of Education*, the U.S. Supreme Court finds that segregation in public schools is unconstitutional, which accelerates the flight of white city residents to the suburbs

1940   **1970**

1965
A race riot in the Watts raises concerns about violence, crime, and poverty in urban African-American neighborhoods; the Voting Rights Act of 1965 outlaws practices designed to restrict African Americans' right to vote

1970
Census information reveals more African Americans are moving from the North to the South, indicating a reverse in earlier migration patterns

1964   The Civil Rights Act of 1964 ends racial segregation in schools, workplaces, and public facilities.

1965   A race riot in the Watts section of Los Angeles, California, raises concerns about violence, crime, and poverty in urban African-American neighborhoods; the Voting Rights Act of 1965 outlaws practices designed to restrict African Americans' right to vote.

1970   Census information reveals more African Americans are moving from the North to the South, indicating a reverse in earlier migration patterns.

Notes

CHAPTER 1

1. Rudolph Fisher, "The City of Refuge," in the *Atlantic Monthly*, February 1925. Available online at http://nationalhumanities center.org/pds/maai3/migrations/ text4/cityofrefuge.pdf.
2. Ibid.
3. Ibid.
4. Ibid.
5. Ibid.
6. Ibid.
7. Ibid.
8. Ibid.
9. Ibid.
10. Ibid.
11. Ibid.

CHAPTER 2

1. Richard Wright, *12 Million Black Voices*, New York, N.Y.: Avalon Publishing Group Inc., 1941, p. 31.
2. "Boley, A Negro Town in the West," In Motion: The African-American Migration Experience, Western Migration. Available online at http://www.inmotion-aame.org/texts/viewer.cfm?id=6_017T&page=430.

CHAPTER 3

1. James N. Gregory, *The Southern Diaspora: How the Great Migrations of Black and White Southerners Transformed America*, Chapel Hill, N.C.: The University of North Carolina Press, 2005, p. 47.
2. Ibid., p. 54.

3. Emmett J. Scott, "Letters of Negro Migrants of 1916–1918," *The Journal of Negro History*, July 1919, pp. 291–292.
4. Ibid., p. 296.
5. Ibid., p. 297.
6. Carole Marks, "The Great Migration: African Americans Searching for the Promised Land, 1916–1930," In Motion: The African-American Migration Experience, The Great Migration. Available online at http://www.inmotionaame.org/texts/viewer.cfm?id=8_000T&page=1

CHAPTER 4

1. Langston Hughes, *The Collected Works of Langston Hughes, Vol. 13: Autobiography: The Big Sea*, Columbia, Mo.: University of Missouri Press, 2003, p. 83.
2. Ibid.
3. Marks, "The Great Migration."

CHAPTER 5

1. Gregory, *The Southern Diaspora*, p. 135.

CHAPTER 6

1. Gregory, *The Southern Diaspora*, p. 29.
2. Ibid., p. 263.
3. Ibid., p. 264.

CHAPTER 7

1. Gregory, *The Southern Diaspora*, p. 273.
2. Ibid., p. 221.

CHAPTER 8

1. Molly Hudgens, "Coming Home Again: African-American Return Migration to the South," In Motion: The African-American Migration Experience, Return South Migration. Available online at http://www.inmotionaame.org/texts/viewer.cfm?id=11_000T&page=1.

2. Gail Russell Chaddock, "How the South Changed," *The Christian Science Monitor*, July 1, 2004. Available online at http://www.csmonitor.com/2004/0701/p01s02-ussc.html.

3. Hudgens, "Coming Home Again."

4. Ibid.

5. Kevin Chappell, "The New Great Migration to the South," *Ebony*, September 1998. Available online at http://findarticles.com/p/articles/mi_m1077/is_n11_v53/ai_21080614/pg_2/?tag=content;col1.

6. Hudgens, "Coming Home Again."

7. Rebecca Leung, "Going Home to the South," 60 Minutes Online, June 15, 2003. Available online at http://www.cbsnews.com/stories/2003/06/12/60minutes/main558375.shtml.

8. Hudgens, "Coming Home Again."

BIBLIOGRAPHY

Dodson, Howard, and Sylviane A. Dioue. *In Motion: The African-American Migration Experience.* Washington, D.C.: National Geographic, 2004.

Frey, William H. "The New Great Migration: Black Americans' Return to the South, 1965–2000," Brookings Census 2000 Series. Washington, D.C.: Brookings Institution Center on Urban & Metropolitan Policy, 2004.

Gregory, James N. *The Southern Diaspora: How the Great Migrations of Black and White Southerners Transformed America.* Chapel Hill, N.C.: The University of North Carolina Press, 2005.

Griffin, Farah Jasmine. *"Who Set You Flowin'?": The African-American Migration Narrative.* New York, N.Y.: Oxford University Press, 1995.

Lemann, Nicholas. *The Promised Land: The Great Black Migration and How It Changed America.* New York, N.Y.: Alfred A. Knopf, 1991.

Marks, Carole. *Farewell—We're Good and Gone: The Great Black Migration.* Bloomington, Ind.: Indiana University Press, 1989.

Reich, Steven A., ed. *Encyclopedia of the Great Black Migration,* Third Ed. Westport, Conn.: Greenwood Press, 2006.

Stack, Carol. *Call to Home: African Americans Reclaim the Rural South.* New York, N.Y.: Basic Books, 1996.

Wright, Richard. *12 Million Black Voices.* New York, N.Y.: Thunder's Mouth Press, 2002.

Further Reading

Candaele, Kerry. *Bound for Glory: From the Great Migration to the Harlem Renaissance, 1910–1930*. New York, N.Y.: Chelsea House, 1996.

Grossman, James R. *A Chance to Make Good: African Americans, 1900–1929*. New York, N.Y.: Oxford University Press, 1997.

Harding, Vincent, et. al. *We Changed the World: African Americans, 1945–1970*. New York, N.Y.: Oxford University Press, 1997.

Haskins, James, and Kathleen Benson. *Out of the Darkness: The Story of Blacks Moving North, 1890–1940*. New York, N.Y.: Benchmark Books, 1999.

Haskins, Jim, ed. *Black Stars of the Harlem Renaissance: African Americans Who Lived Their Dreams*. New York, N.Y.: John Wiley, 2002.

Hill, Laban Carrick. *Harlem Stomp!: A Cultural History of the Harlem Renaissance*. New York, N.Y.: Little Brown, 2003.

McNeese, Tim. *The Civil Rights Movement: Striving for Justice*. New York, N.Y.: Chelsea House, 2008.

Trotter, Joe William, Jr. *From a Raw Deal to a New Deal?: African Americans, 1929–1945*. New York, N.Y.: Oxford University Press, 1996.

Uschan, Michael V. *Lynching and Murder in the Deep South*. San Diego, Calif.: Lucent Books, 2006.

———. *Reconstruction*. San Diego, Calif.: Lucent Books, 2007.

WEB SITES
The African-American Mosaic: Migrations
http://www.loc.gov/exhibits/african/afam008.html

Part of the Library of Congress Resource Guide for the Study of
    Black History and Culture, this site features maps, documents,
    and photographs relating to the migrations of southern African
    Americans to Kansas in the late nineteenth century and to Chi-
    cago, Illinois, in the early twentieth century.

In Motion: The African-American Migration Experience

http://www.inmotionaame.org

This invaluable resource, created by the New York Public
    Library's Schomburg Center for Research in Black Culture,
    explores in depth various migrations of African Americans
    throughout history, including the Great Migration, Second Great
    Migration, and the Great Migration South (called the Return
    South Migration on this Web site).

The Making of African American Identity: Vol. III, 1917–1968: Migrations

http://www.nationalhumanitiescenter.org/pds/maai3/migrations/
    migrations.htm

In this Web site, the National Humanities Center presents a com-
    pilation of primary sources dealing with the various migrations
    of black Americans during the twentieth century.

North by South

http://northbysouth.kenyon.edu

Created by students at Kenyon College, this site focuses on the
    migration of rural Southern blacks to northern cities between
    1900 and 1960.

The Rise and Fall of Jim Crow

http://www.pbs.org/wnet/jimcrow/index.html

Tied into a series aired on the Public Broadcasting Service
    (PBS), this Web site includes a timeline of the Jim Crow era in
    the American South and personal narratives of African Ameri-
    cans who lived during this period.

PHOTO CREDITS

INDEX

A

Abbott, Robert S., 27, 30, 33
advertisements, 33
Agricultural Adjustment Act, 62–63
air conditioning, 90
Ali, Noble Drew, 58
Alston, Charles, 66
American Colonization Society, 21
Amos and Andy (radio show), 55–56
Amsterdam News, 65
Angelou, Maya, 94
Armstrong, Louis, 53
Atlanta, Georgia, 93, 95–96, 102–104
Atlanta Independent, 27
Atlantic Monthly, 1
auto industry in Detroit, 87

B

Baptist churches, 49, 56, 101
baseball leagues, African-American, 55
Bearden, Romare, 66
Black Belt, 98
blues, 52–53, 54, 100
Boley, Oklahoma, 20–21
boll weevil, 18
"Bound for the Promised Land" (poem), 28–30
boycotts, 105
Brown, Claude, 76–77
The Builders (Lawrence), 67
Bureau of Refugees, Freedmen, and Abandoned Lands, 11

businesses, black-owned
  entrepreneurs, 99
  in Harlem, 46–47
  newspapers, 27–34, 65, 80–81, 105

C

characteristics of migrants, 36–38
Chicago Defender, 27–34, 65, 81
Chicago race riots (Red Summer of 1919), 45, 48
Chicago Urban League, 42
churches, black, 34, 49, 56–58, 82–83, 101
"City of Refuge" (Fisher), 1–6
Civil Rights Act (1875), 11
Civil Rights Act (1964), 85, 90
civil rights movement
  affect on the South, 90
  laws passed as a result of, 85
  Northern roots of, 104–105
  strategies, 82
Congress, blacks elected to, 11, 60, 104
Congress of Racial Equality (CORE), 82
Constitution, U.S., 11
contracts for sharecropping, 18
CORE (Congress of Racial Equality), 82
Cotton Club, 55
The Crisis, 82
Cullen, Countee, 51
culture, southern, 49

D

Davis, Elijah, 91
deindustrialization, 87
Democratic Party, 85
Denby, Charles, 65
DePriest, Oscar Stanton, 60
Detroit Riot (1943), 69–71
disease, 45
Divine, Father, 58
Douglass, Frederick, 67
Du Bois, W. E. B., 6

E

Ebony, 82
Ellison, Ralph, 66
Emancipation Proclamation, 10
emigrationism, 21
employers, 42, 48
employment
    after World War II, 75
    deindustrialization, 87
    federal ban on discrimination
        in, 67–68
    opportunities in the North,
        42–43
    recruiting and recruiters, 23,
        25–26, 33
    in Sunbelt, 89
    unemployment during
        Depression, 61
    World War I and, 24–25
    World War II and, 63, 68–69
empowerment, black, 58–59
entertainment as enticement to
    migrate, 31. *See also* music
European immigration, 25
Executive Order 8802, 67–68
Exodusters, 18–21

F

family ties, 91–94
Fard, Wallace D., 58

Federal Home Administration
    (FHA), 75
Fifteenth Amendment, 11
Fisher, Rudolph, 5–6
Ford Motor Company, 42
Fort Huachuca, Arizona, 69
Foster, Nancy, 92
Foster, Rube, 55
Fourteenth Amendment, 11
Franklin, C. L., 83
Franklin, David McCoy, 102
Franklin, Shirley, 102–104
Freedmen's Bureau, 11
Freeman, Morgan, 92–93

G

Garvey, Marcus, 58–59
GI Bill, 74
government jobs, 75
Great Depression, 8, 61–63
Great Migration, 8, 97
Great Migration South, 86–87,
    97, 101
"Great Northern Drive," 31
Great Society programs, 87

H

Harlem, 1–6, 39–40, 45, 46–47
Harlem Renaissance, 5–6, 50–51,
    99
Hartt, Rollin Lynde, 46
health, 45
hip-hop, 100
Home Owner's Loan Corpora-
    tion, 75–76
Horne, Mother Rosa, 58
housing, 43–45, 48, 75–79, 88
Hughes, Langston, 39–40, 51, 66
Hurston, Zora Neale, 51

I

"I'd Like to Show You Harlem!"
    (Hartt), 46–47

The Independent (magazine), 46
inner cities, 79–80
International Migration Society, 21
Islam, 58

J
Jackson, Maynard, 103
jazz, 51–53, 100
Jet, 82
Jim Crow, 11–13
jobs. *See* employment
Johnson, James Weldon, 45
Johnson, John H., 81–82

K
Kansas, 19–20
King, Martin Luther, Jr., 89, 90
Kingdom and Peace Mission, New York, 58
Knight, Gwendolyn, 67
Ku Klux Clan, 14

L
labor agents, 26, 33
labor unions, 43, 62
Lawrence, Jacob, 66–67
letters, 33–34
Liberia, 21
Los Angeles, 88–89
lynchings, 1, 14–15, 16

M
magazines, 46, 56, 82, 105
Manchild in the Promised Land (Brown), 76–77
Mays, Marguerite, 79
Mays, Willie, 79
McIlherron, Jim, 16–17
McKay, Claude, 51
media attention, national, 56
Methodist churches, 56–57

migrants
    characteristics of, 36–38
    help for newcomers, 40–42
    letters from, 34
    tensions with older residents, 48–49
migration clubs, 34–35
The Migration of the Negro (Lawrence), 66–67
military, African Americans in, 69
Molpus, Dick, 90
money
    high rents, 45
    incentives to earn, 42–43
    sent back home to the South, 34
    for traveling north, 35
    wages, 43
Moorish Science Temple, 58
music, 51–55, 99–100
Muslims, 58

N
Nation of Islam, 58
National Association for the Advancement of Colored People (NAACP), 16, 82
National Urban League, New York, 42
Native Son (Wright), 80
Negro Digest, 81
neighborhoods and communities, black, 31, 43–45, 50, 80
New Bethel Baptist Church, Detroit, 83
New Deal policies, 62, 85
New York City. *See* Harlem
newspapers
    black-owned, 27–34, 65, 80–81, 105
    white, 26–27
nightclubs, 54–55

93rd Infantry Division, 69
Nixon, Richard, 87

O

Obama, Barack, 104
Oklahoma Territory, 20–21
Olivet Baptist Church, Chicago,
  56

P

Pacific Coast, 68–69, 74–75
pay, 43
Pennsylvania Railroad Company,
  23
Plessy, Homer A., 13
Plessy v. Ferguson (1896), 13
police harassment, 45
political activism, black, 82–85.
  See also civil rights movement
politicians, black, 11, 60, 101–104
poverty, urban, 87–88
pride, racial, 47, 58
public housing, 88

R

race riots. *See* riots
radio, 55–56
Rainey, Gertrude "Ma," 52
Randolph, A. Philip, 65
rappers, 100
Reconstruction, 11, 14, 17, 21
recruiting and recruiters, 23,
  25–26, 33
Red Summer (1919), 45–48
redlining, 77–78
religion, 34, 49, 56–58, 82–83, 101
Republican Party, 85
restrictive covenants, 78
retirement to the South, 91–93
Rice, Thomas "Daddy," 12
riots
  Detroit Riot (1943), 69–71
  King assassination and, 89

Red Summer (1919), 45–48
Watts Riot (1965), 88–89
Robeson, Paul, 51
Robinson, Ida, 58
Roosevelt, Franklin D., 62, 66–68,
  70, 85

S

schools, segregated, 13
"Second Emancipation," 31
Second Great Migration, 8,
  72–74, 97
segregation, racial, 13
service organizations, African
  American, 42
sharecroppers, 16–18, 62–63
Shelley v. Kramer (1948), 78
Singleton, Benjamin "Pap,"
  18–20
sit-ins, 82, 105
Smith, Bessie, 52–53
Smith, Earnest, 89
Smith, Lucy, 58
Smith, Marnie, 54
soldiers, African-American, 69
the South
  black remaining in, after Civil
    War, 10–11
  decision and strategies to
    leave, 35–36
  desire of blacks to escape,
    6–7
  Jim Crow, rise of, 11–13
  migration back to, 86–96
southern culture, 49
Southern Tenant Farmers'
  Union, 62
sports, 55
suburbanization, 79–80
Sunbelt, 89–90, 96
sunset towns, 13–14
Supreme Court, U.S., 13, 78
Sweet, Ossian, 43

T
Thirteenth Amendment, 11
Thomas, Renee, 95–96
Thompson, William Hale, 60
Toomer, Jean, 51
torture, 16–17
train porters, 32
train travel, 35, 36
Tubman, Harriet, 67
Turner, Henry McNeal, 21

U
unions, 43, 62
Universal Negro Improvement
    Association (UNIA), 58–59
urban poor, 87–88
urbanization, 98–99

V
veterans, black, 74, 75
violence
    Detroit Riot (1943), 69–71
    King assassination, riots
        following, 89

Ku Klux Clan, 14
lynchings, 1, 14–15, 16
McIlherron murder, 16–17
Red Summer (1919), 45–48
Watts Riot (1965), 88–89
voting rights, 13–14, 101
Voting Rights Act (1965), 85,
    101

W
wages, 43
Washington, Booker T., 20
Watts Riot (1965), 88–89
West, migration to, 68–69,
    74–75
White, Walter F., 65–66
white flight, 79–80
William, Eugene, 45, 48
Willis, Etta, 91
Winbush, Raymond, 96
women, 74
World War I, 24–25
World War II, 63, 68–69, 72
Wright, Richard, 80

ABOUT THE AUTHOR

LIZ SONNEBORN is a freelance writer living in Brooklyn, New York. A graduate of Swarthmore College, she has written more than 80 books for children and adults. Her works include *The End of Apartheid in South Africa*, *The American West*, *The Gold Rush*, *Yemen*, *A to Z of American Indian Women*, and *The Ancient Kushites*, which the African Studies Association's Children's Africana Book Awards named an Honor Book for Older Readers in 2006.